Sylvester's JOURNAL

Scrawled secrets. A heart sealed
off from wife and God . . .
Was his life a sham?

LESTER BAUMAN

ISBN: 978-1-949648-93-5

Cover artist: Peter Balholm

Cover and text layout design: Kristi Yoder

Second printing: October 2020

Printed in the USA

Published by:
TGS International
P.O. Box 355
Berlin, Ohio 44610 USA
Phone: 330.893.4828
Fax: 330.893.2305
www.tgsinternational.com

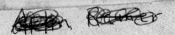

Sylvester's JOURNAL

Just think, some night the stars will gleam
Upon a cold grey stone,
And trace a name with silver beam,
And lo! 'twill be your own.
—Robert W. Service, "Just Think!"

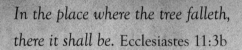

In the place where the tree falleth,
there it shall be. Ecclesiastes 11:3b

LESTER BAUMAN

Table of Contents

Introduction

This book takes place in the 1870s in a large Mennonite community in the eastern part of North America. Spiritually, the Mennonite Church was in a low period during this time. They considered the Methodists to be their enemies, since some "spiritually-minded" younger Mennonite families had gone over to them.

In some cases, terminology has changed from then until now. The New Birth, for instance, was viewed more as something that one grew into, rather than the impulsive, revival meeting type of conversion experience common in the Methodist settings of the time. Even today, there are Old Order Mennonites who, though they are obviously Christians, cannot tell you the day or the hour they decided to follow Jesus.

The idea of a confessional journal as portrayed in this book will be a little strange to many readers. Though in this story it is the product of my imagination, such journals were actually written, mostly in small offshoots of the mainstream Mennonites, like the Reformed Mennonites.

In some ways, this book is fiction, but in other ways it isn't. Some of the strangest incidents in the book were derived from actual happenings. (Any exact likeness to people alive today is coincidental and unintended.) Even with the higher levels of accountability in today's church settings, people do go astray. Some of these people try to hide their sin. And hidden sin always has repercussions, not only for the people committing it, but also for their family, friends, and church. Hopefully, this book will reveal some of these repercussions.

—Lester Bauman

Prologue

The wilted grass growing along the rail fence that surrounded the old graveyard bore testimony to the day's pressing heat. Soon the sun would sink out of sight in the west, and even now a quiet breeze had sprung up, bringing a measure of relief. Except for the twittering of sparrows and the cry of a mourning dove, nothing disturbed the sleep of the ones buried in those serene depths. The raw wound close to the fence, partially concealed with fresh soil, was the only evidence of the somber ceremony that had taken place in the old graveyard that day; nothing remained of the swarming crowd who had witnessed it.

The breeze picked up as the sun sank lower, and it began to moan through the willow trees in the fencerow. The shadows cast by the bare branches of several half-dead oak trees crept slowly across the graveyard as the twilight deepened. Something was wrong, and even nature seemed to sense it.

Who was buried there?

PART 1

Andrew's Perspective

I struggled with bad attitudes toward my father Sylvester when I was young. This struggle came back to haunt me as I stood beside his coffin and looked at him for the last time. I vowed to make sure none of my children would ever feel like that when they stood beside my coffin.

Thankfully, my wife helped me find my way through this, as you'll see. Most of all, God helped me by showing me that this was my problem just as much as my father's problem. Bishop George helped a lot too. He has long been a close friend of our family, though he died before this book was published.

Twenty-five years have passed since my father's death. I've put most of it behind me now. But recently we've been hearing of other fathers caught in a trap like my father was. And I'm sure there are some out there keeping it hidden, like my father did. As a family, we decided to ask someone to write the story of my father's life and the repercussions it had on us.

I hope this story can help some other people find their way before it's too late for them. For my father, it is too late.

Andrew Martin

Andrew Visits His Mother

1

People think I'm a hard man. But someday I'll be gone and they will
realize what I've done for them all these years . . .
—Sylvester Martin

Andrew paused to glance at the calendar before opening
the screen door to head for the barn. No one had torn off the old
month, so he reached up and pulled off the sheet. The bold black
lettering shouted at him, **August 1876**.

"As if I could ever forget," he muttered. Only a week ago they had
buried his father, and the responsibility of looking after his mother
and sisters had descended on his shoulders. They were broad shoulders and strong enough by all appearances. But one glance at his
youthful face was enough to tell anyone he was too young for this
responsibility. At least his family was small; both of his sisters worked
as maids in the church community, and his mother lived alone. His
parents had married later than most and his mother was already
fifty-six, even though her only son, the oldest child, was less than
thirty years old.

Who would have expected that his father, Sylvester Martin—well-known carpenter and local Mennonite cabinet maker—would fall over because of an apoplexy, a stroke, at fifty-seven years old?

I should have known that his temper would do him in someday. Andrew's thoughts churned as he strode across the well-kept yard toward the sturdy barn to hitch his horse. *But of all things, for it to happen during a meeting with the ministers.* He shook his head. He knew word had started to trickle through the church community about the circumstances of his father's death, even though the ministers and the family had tried to keep it quiet. Ignoring the obvious evidence, the local minister worked hard to persuade the hundreds of people at the funeral that their "beloved brother" Sylvester was now sleeping quietly and only awaited the last judgment to usher him into the bliss of glory.[1]

Andrew pulled his horse and buggy to a stop beside the clapboard-sided house. Its builders had crafted the house as carefully as they had the barn and driving shed across the yard. The former owners of the house had even painted it sometime in the last decade, which was unusual for a farmhouse during that era. Andrew wasn't thinking of buildings today, however. His face relaxed for the first time that afternoon as Selina stepped nimbly into the buggy.

"Ready to go?" he smiled at his wife, then loosened the reins and clicked his tongue to the horse.

Selina was wearing a black dress, of course. The community would expect her to do so for at least a year every time she left home, as a way of giving proper respect to her father-in-law. But the somber color couldn't hide her beauty, and the curly blond hair that peeked from her bonnet defied any idea of somberness. Her smile twinkled at Andrew with a delight that five years of childless marriage hadn't managed to suppress.

But she sobered quickly as she remembered their errand. "How

---

[1] It was common for Old Mennonites to believe in "soul sleep" or Christian Mortalism.

do you suppose your mother is doing?" She asked the question hesitantly, not wanting to disturb his pleasure in her presence.

Andrew's smile faded. "Well, you know my mother," he said. "She will submit to this as being God's plan for her, just as she did with every other event involving my father over the years. She always found it easier to accept things than I did."

It was only a few miles to the small farm where Naomi Martin now lived by herself. She had seen them drive in the lane, and stepped out onto the front porch to greet them. Andrew tied his horse to the hitching post and loosened the checkrein that held up the horse's head during normal driving. Selina didn't wait for him, but walked up the hard-packed dirt walkway to the worn wooden porch steps. Her mother-in-law met her there.

Andrew grimaced slightly as he saw the stiff handshake they gave each other. *It's a wonder Selina didn't give her a hug*, he thought. *But she must have remembered that it isn't proper to show emotion, even to your mother-in-law.* He knew how his wife felt about the Old Mennonite practices, but he also knew that she respected Naomi too much to breach them at a time like this. He couldn't help but compare the two women as he walked toward the house. Like Selina, his mother was slender. Her black hair showed a touch of grey, though she had neatly tucked it under the plain cloth head covering designated by the church. His mother used to be a spirited person, and that still showed somewhat in the way she held her head, but the burden of years of marriage had worn her down.

Andrew formally shook his mother's hand and gave her the standard German greeting, "*Wie geht's?*"[2] No one expected a literal answer to the rhetorical question, especially at a time like this. His mother

---

[2] Literal translation: *How goes?*

shook his hand warmly, but her reply caught in her throat. Silently, she turned toward the house, motioning them to follow her.

Andrew and Selina seated themselves at the worn wooden table while Naomi put water on for tea.

"It's almost too hot to keep a fire burning." Her statement was an attempt to fill the silence and no one answered. After the first awkward moments, everyone relaxed, and they discussed the recent events.

"Did you have any idea that Father wasn't well?" Selina asked. "It happened so suddenly."

Naomi shook her head. "I never thought of it at all," she answered. "He went to town that last afternoon to see a customer, just as he often did. He seemed a bit upset when he realized Bishop George and Preacher Daniel wanted to have a meeting with him. Other than that, I never noticed anything out of the ordinary."

Naomi paused, and then continued to talk about that last evening with her husband. Andrew could picture it as she spoke . . .

Naomi walked to the window for the third time. "I hope Sylvester gets home before Bishop George and Preacher Daniel get here," she said, half to herself. Sylvester often left his business contacts for later in the day. Naomi had already finished the few chores they had. Supper waited on the table, but there was still no sight of Sylvester.

She walked back to the stove and stirred the potato soup to keep it from burning, then returned to her post by the window. "I do hope he didn't stop for a glass with someone." Naomi was clearly uneasy. Sylvester wasn't a heavy drinker, but like many Mennonite men of the time, he did enjoy a glass of hard cider and a cigar or a chew of tobacco with a friend on occasion. Hopefully this trip to town hadn't turned into one of those occasions.

A crease formed between Naomi's brows. She wondered again what the bishop and minister wanted to talk to Sylvester *about. Bishop George had seemed uncomfortable when he stopped in a few hours earlier to tell Naomi that they were coming. Sylvester had just left for town, so George left a message with her. Now she wished she had warned him that Sylvester might be late.*

She stirred the soup again. Returning to the window one more time, she heard a buggy turning into the lane, and she quickened her steps. "Good, it's Sylvester." She exhaled sharply as she recognized the horse, only then realizing she had been holding her breath.

Sylvester was just barely in time, however. Bishop George and Preacher Daniel turned into the lane just as Sylvester jumped from his buggy to unhitch his horse.

". . . and that's about all I know," Naomi concluded. "The three of them came into the house together and went straight to the parlor for their meeting. They closed the door behind them."

Andrew's mind had been wandering, as his eyes traveled idly around the familiar surroundings. This was the room he had missed the most after he left home. The dark hardwood floor, the old black cook stove, and the worn daybed on the far side of the room all brought back old memories.

"Do you have any idea what the meeting was about?" His voice shook a bit. "Or what upset Father so badly? It must have been something serious. I mean, we all knew he had a problem with his temper, but to get so angry that he had an apoplexy was . . ." he faltered.

Naomi shook her head. "No one told me what was going on," she answered quietly. "They might tell you if you were to ask them. You are the oldest son, and they would probably think you had the right to know." Her shoulders sagged. "I really don't think they were being that hard on him, at least not without reason. They aren't the kind to be abusive." She took a deep breath and another sip of tea. "Both were very apologetic and did their best to help me. And Preacher Daniel's funeral message was very kind."

Andrew pursed his lips, irritably. "I wonder how much he believed the wonderful things he said," he replied cynically. "And I wonder what people were thinking while he said them."

"Well, we don't want to speak ill of God's servants," his mother answered softly. "And God knows your father did many good things during his time with us. We must remember those things and hope for the best."[3]

Andrew contemplated saying more, but he caught his wife's warning glance and changed the subject. "Do you know anything about Dad's financial affairs? Are there any bills that need to be paid? Does anyone owe him money?"

"He never told me much," his mother answered. "But he kept everything in his desk in the parlor, as you know.[4] He always kept the key in his pocket, but I took it out before they took away the body. I'll get it for you."

Andrew and Selina glanced at each other as Naomi stepped into the bedroom and returned with a black wrought-iron key. "He never wanted me to meddle," she explained apologetically. "So I thought I would leave it for you to go through his desk and see if anything needs to be looked after."

Andrew was inserting the key into the desk when he heard buggy wheels in the lane. "Who is that?" He paused, then slipped the key into his pocket. He turned from the desk, half relieved at the interruption. His father had never allowed him to meddle with the desk either, and it seemed as if he was transgressing to do so even now.

"It's your sisters," his mother exclaimed from the window. "I'm surprised they both had time to come today again. It's canning season."

Martha and Hettie had hardly joined the sober group around the table when another buggy came up the lane.

---

[3] This was a standard Mennonite sentiment of the times.

[4] Parlors at that time were a separate room, closed off during the week in most homes. The kitchen served as dining room and living room as well as kitchen, and was the largest room in the house. A large roll-top or flip-top desk, kept either in the master bedroom or the parlor, was standard furniture in most middle-class homes.

"Now who?" frowned Andrew, pulling back the curtain to look out. "Why, it's Bishop George and Sister Nancy. I wonder what they want." His heart pounded a bit as he headed out the door to help them find a place to tie their horse in the now crowded area in front of the little house.

The bishop was a kindly-looking older man, somewhat plump, with a curly gray beard and a friendly personality. But he looked grave as he and his wife courteously accepted chairs at the table, and cups of tea. He got to the point right away.

"I suppose you are wondering why we are here," Bishop George said. "Normally our deacon would check to make sure you were looked after financially. I'm sure he will be around to talk to you soon. But I thought we would drop in to make sure you weren't in need of anything." He glanced at Andrew. "I'm sure Andrew is looking into that as well. We want to be sure that either of you feels free to let us know of any needs you might have."

He hesitated, and glanced at his wife. "But we also wanted to talk with you about what happened the evening Sylvester died. I was going to stop in and see you as well, Andrew. But now that all of you are here, I won't need to do that."

His voice trailed away, and he cleared his throat awkwardly, then hitched his chair a couple of inches closer to the table.

"Sylvester wasn't very happy to see us, as you probably realized," he said to Naomi. He waited until she nodded, then continued. "It is unfortunate that he didn't have more time to get himself pulled together for the meeting. As it was, the whole evening seemed to get off on the wrong foot."

He shifted unhappily on his stiff wooden chair, clearing his throat again. He took a deep breath. "We came to share a concern with him about some of his business practices," he said. "We had been getting complaints from some of the church people about things they kept hearing from others. And the day before our meeting, the black-smith in town told me that Sylvester had built him a cabinet that was mostly pine, when he had ordered oak and paid for oak. Sylvester claimed that he had quoted the price for pine, but the blacksmith and his wife both clearly remembered he had promised them oak.

"If this had been the only such incident, we would have chalked it up to a misunderstanding, but unfortunately it wasn't." The bishop took another sip of tea and shook his head at Naomi's unspoken offer of a refill. "I won't go into all the details here, but it was clear that Sylvester's word no longer meant much to him, and something needed to be done."

"Unfortunately, Sylvester took our visit as a personal affront, which I guess it was, actually." He glanced at Naomi apologetically, and then lowered his eyes to the dark tablecloth. "I knew he had a bit of a problem with his temper, but I had never witnessed it before. You probably heard him, even though the parlor door was closed."

The bishop glanced at Naomi again, and she nodded, brushing a tear from the corner of her eye.

Andrew had been watching and listening, dismayed but not sur-prised at this revelation of his father's actions. He had known all too well about his father's temper—he could still remember some of the bruises he had suffered from the black leather strap hanging in the barn. *I wonder if that strap is still out there.* It was not a good thought; irritated at himself, he brought his mind back to the discussion.

"Preacher Daniel tried to calm him down, but he just got more upset," Bishop George added. He hesitated, reluctant to continue, knowing the pain his words would cause. "It almost seemed as if the hand of God struck him down at that moment. He was actu-ally in the middle of swearing at Daniel, when a strange look came over his face and he stuttered incoherently. He tried to steady him-self, but he had lost his coordination and he sort of slid down and then slumped to the floor." An echo of the awe Bishop George had felt lingered in his voice.

"That was when we came for you," the bishop finished. "And you know the rest of the story. He was dead before the doctor got here."

Naomi wiped her eyes again, and a sob escaped through her lips. "He never had a chance to say goodbye to me, or even to pray. His last words on earth were curse words." Andrew could see the pain her statement caused her. "I have wondered ever since . . . Does he— can he—have any chance of going to heaven if he died like that?" The question seemed forced, as if she feared to hear the answer. "I remember the things Daniel said at his funeral, but I can't help wondering . . ."

The room was deadly quiet as the reality of what she was asking sank in. Andrew had been struggling with similar thoughts, even before this latest revelation. He looked at the bishop, anxious to hear his response. The bishop clearly wished he was somewhere else— *probably anywhere else*, Andrew thought, suddenly pitying him. *He has doubtless struggled with the same question.*

Bishop George squared his shoulders. "I don't know," he admitted. Then he echoed Naomi's earlier words. "We can only hope. We have a merciful heavenly Father. We all have failings, and God will make all things clear at the judgment."[5]

The room went quiet again as they digested his words. Everyone jumped a little as a knot of firewood cracked in the woodstove. The suspense broken, the bishop nodded to Sister Nancy and got to his feet, then abruptly sat down again.

"We need to leave," he said, "but I'd like to pray with you before we go." He pulled a German New Testament from his pocket. "Let me read a few words of comfort first."

Andrew followed Bishop George and his wife to their buggy and untied their horse for them before walking to the side of the buggy

---

[5] This is not the answer we would expect today, and some readers may flinch at this. It is, however, a correct picture of what the Mennonite Church would have taught at the time.

to shake the bishop's hand. But he hesitated there, and the bishop waited for him to say what was on his mind.

"Should we go around and make some of my father's wrongs right?" Andrew shifted from one foot to the other. "I think he probably left enough money that we could do that."

The bishop pondered this question for a moment. "I actually thought of that," he admitted. "Maybe the church could help as well, to show the community we do not agree with such business practices. And to make sure it doesn't become a hardship for your mother."

He loosened the reins, and the horse started off. "Leave it with me," he called back over his shoulder. "I'll talk to Preacher Daniel about it. We'll get back to you soon."

Andrew stood in the lane, shoulders sagging, watching them leave. Then he turned back to the house.

Finding the Book

2

Some people have no respect for a hardworking man. They're always
finding fault with him or going against his wishes.
—Sylvester Martin

Naomi was adding more wood to the fire in the old cast-iron cookstove when Andrew walked back into the kitchen. "All of you are welcome to stay for supper if you have time," she said. "I can peel some potatoes for potato soup."

Martha and Hettie looked at each other and Martha glanced at the clock. "It's almost 4:30," she gasped. "I must get supper ready at home. We need to go right away."

Andrew caught Selina's attention across the table after his sisters had left. "We don't really need to be home for anything, do we?" It was more of a statement than a question, but he still waited until she nodded in agreement. "I'd like to see what I can find in Dad's desk about his financial affairs before we go, and that might take a while."

Selina and Naomi started peeling potatoes for supper, chatting companionably about their gardens and the weather. Andrew watched them for a few minutes. *It's good we're staying. This will get my mother's thoughts away from what she just heard.* Reluctantly he pulled the black wrought-iron key from his pocket. *I guess I can't put it off any longer. I hope I don't get any more surprises.*

It only took a few minutes to unlock the old wooden desk and roll up the top, exposing the neatly-sorted contents inside. *I'll start here; he used to keep old files and furniture blueprints in the drawers below. For a man, he sure kept a tidy desk.*

He soon found what he was looking for—a leather bound ledger filled with figures, neatly inscribed in ink. With it was a bank book, showing a balance of over $15,000; enough to take care of his mother for a long time. *If we don't have to give it all to his unhappy customers.* The thought was involuntary, and he looked at the figures again. *I wonder if there is any way to know who all was involved. That could make things tight for us. I wonder if he had any other bank accounts.*

He started to look for more bank books or some sign that his father might have kept cash in the desk. He pulled open a drawer, and then he discovered it—an old black book that someone had handled a lot over the years. Curious, he pulled it out and opened it, flipping through the pages. It was full of his father's handwriting, again in ink. He read a few sentences, and then stopped short, realizing that this could be the surprise he had feared he would find.

A journal.

He was thoughtfully flipping the pages with his thumb when Selina came to the door to call him for supper. She noticed the book he was holding and stepped up beside him. "What is that?" She asked the question hesitantly, noting the look on his face.

"My father kept a journal," he replied slowly. He turned the worn book over in his hands. "I was trying to decide if I should read it or if we would be better off just throwing it away."

Selina caught her breath as the implication sank in. "Do you suppose . . . ?"

"I don't know. I haven't really read much in it, just something about some nails he bought, but he dated the entries. It starts way back before he and Mother were married." Andrew flipped to the last page with writing on it. "Look, he wrote in it the night before he died. It is definitely a journal, or a record book of some sort."

They looked at each other, neither one wanting to be first to read the book that Andrew carefully closed. "We'd better talk to Mother about it," Andrew finally said. "Maybe she will want to read it first. At least she should help decide what to do about it."

Naomi blinked in surprise when they showed her the journal. She took it carefully when Andrew offered it to her, but she didn't open it.

"I wonder why Sylvester never told me about this," she said softly. "I knew he often spent time at his desk. He always had his desk in the parlor, and he kept the door closed when he was in there. He got upset if I bothered him or walked in while he was working there. I've never seen this book."

Naomi handed the journal back to Andrew. "You decide what to do with it," she said. "Sylvester didn't want me to read it, evidently, and I'll stay faithful to that. But someone should read it, just in case . . ." She trailed off helplessly, not knowing how to put into words what they all feared.

Andrew understood. Even though Sylvester was gone, and she had just learned the ugly truth of how he had died, she was still faithful to him. The book might very well confirm the fears she had often fought, even while he was still living. Andrew was sure of one thing: his mother wouldn't be reading the journal.

Naomi finally broke the silence again. "I think you should read it, or at least skim through it," she told Andrew. "It might tell us how we could go about making his wrongs right. And there might be more wrongs that we don't know about. If there is enough money, I would like to do that for him."

"He left enough money to keep you in comfort for the rest of your life," Andrew said. "His bank account has over $15,000 dollars in it. But if we start paying large sums, it might make life difficult for you."

Naomi straightened her back, and they saw a flash of the determination that had brought her through many tough times. "I will not live in comfort with money stolen from my neighbors," she answered firmly. "I would live off charity before I did that."

Andrew nodded. "You will live comfortably as long as I can provide for you," he promised. "Bishop George said the church might want to help with some of the restitution. He thought it would help to clear up the bad testimony Father left."

Naomi bowed her head. "All this time, we were cheating people, and I didn't know it. How will I ever face people again?" She covered her face with her hands. "I knew that Sylvester had his failings, but I never knew he wasn't honest in his business dealings," she cried painfully. Andrew and Selina stared at the floor as the widow regained control.

Naomi followed them to the door, laying her hand on Andrew's arm to stop him. "Please, if you do read your father's journal and find something that I should know," her voice broke a bit, "then please tell me, even if it hurts."

Andrew stared at his mother, frowning. *I think she suspects more than she has told us. I wonder what all she went through with my father that the rest of us never knew about.* He jerked a nod in agreement and strode out the door.

Later that evening, after he had finished his chores, Andrew sat by his desk in the bedroom. Selina, sensitive to his feelings, left him to face "the book" alone. Slowly he reached out, as if expecting a scorpion sting, and flipped back the cover. He saw the inscription on the flyleaf for the first time.

This is my private journal and is to be burned at my death. May God have mercy on my soul.

—Sylvester Martin

It took Andrew a few moments to grasp the significance of what he had just read. He got up and walked to the bedroom door, leaning on the jamb for support.

"Selina," he called, his voice shaking. Selina looked up from her reading at the kitchen table, alarmed at the tone of his voice. Quickly she jumped to her feet and went to him, grasping him by the arm.

"What's wrong?" Her eyes searched his, looking for a clue to his sudden agitation.

Wordlessly Andrew led his wife into the bedroom and showed her the inscription on the flyleaf. "Now what do I do? Do I follow his instructions and burn it, or do I read it?"

Selina read the inscription several times before answering slowly. "But if you don't read it, you will always wonder what he didn't want anyone to know." She hesitated a bit. "And how will you know whom he cheated, if you don't read it?"

Andrew bit his lip, a habit he had when he was agitated. "I know. But if I do read it, I will always feel that I disrespected him. I want to honor him despite what he was."

Selina spread her hands helplessly. "I guess I don't know what you should do. Talk to your mother about it. Or Bishop George. Either way, it's too late to do anything about it tonight. Why don't we just go to bed and sleep over it before deciding?"

The next morning, right after breakfast and the morning chores, Andrew hitched up his horse and drove to Bishop George's house. Selina stayed home to work in the garden while Andrew sorted out what to do with the journal.

Bishop George was home. He looked troubled, opening the book gingerly and looking at the inscription on the flyleaf as Andrew poured out the story of how he had found it.

Andrew watched him from across the table without commenting. *We all do that. We treat that book as if it might blow up in our faces. It's just an innocent-looking journal. But is it innocent? I guess that's the problem.*

The bishop closed the book without reading further. He closed his eyes for a moment, then sat back in his chair as if he had made up his mind. "I think you should read it," he said. "I didn't tell your mother everything I've heard about your father. I think it would be good if we could either prove or disprove some of those stories and lay them to rest."

His voice softened as he continued sympathetically. "But let me warn you that it may not be easy. As I said, I've heard some stories. Of course, they may be just false rumors. I don't need to know everything you find, but if it becomes too much for you, feel free to come back and share. It may be a heavy burden."

"Our actions have repercussions," he added. "Our failures create burdens for our families to bear. Your mother does not need to have this load on top of her widowhood."

The sorrow in the bishop's eyes lingered in Andrew's mind for a long time. He realized his father's actions had not only affected his mother's load but also added to the load the bishop carried. It gave him a lot to think about while he drove down the road. *Even the church suffers when something like this happens. I hope I never cause Selina the heartache my mother is going through.*

Selina had a late lunch ready by the time Andrew returned home. He toyed with his food moodily. "I'm glad it rained overnight," he said. "I need to mow that third cutting of hay in the back field, but

I sure don't feel like it. It looks like it might rain again anyway. I think I'll just leave it for today."

He hadn't mentioned the journal, though Selina noticed he had brought it back and laid it carefully on his desk. They finished their potato soup and beans in silence. Andrew was spooning applesauce onto a piece of buttered bread when Selina finally brought up the subject. "Have you decided what to do with the journal?" she asked timidly.

He took a bite of bread and applesauce. "I talked to Bishop George, and he felt I should read it, even though I probably won't like what I find. I guess I'll go ahead and read it."

He laid down his spoon on the table with a clatter as if to emphasize what he was going to say. "I sincerely hope I *never* put you—or our children, if we ever have any—through the kind of pressure this is putting on our family." He glared at the applesauce as if it personally carried the blame for his feelings.

Selina reached across the table and took his hand in hers. "Andrew," she said earnestly, "I am not in the least worried that you will ever do that. You are as different from your father as night is different from day."

Andrew looked sheepishly at her. "I guess that was a stupid thing to get upset at. But Bishop George talked a bit about the selfishness of allowing the burden of our failures to fall on others. I had never really thought of it from that perspective. My sins can harm others just as much as they harm me."

He started to eat again. "I really thought I had gotten over my bitterness about how my father treated me while I was growing up." He sighed. "Now I've got to go through it all over again."

Andrew spent the afternoon working on his haying equipment so it would be ready to go in the morning, if the weather held. But it was easy to see his heart wasn't in it. That is, it would have been easy to see if there had been someone to watch him, which there wasn't. Not unless you counted the black tomcat that kept trying to rub against his leg. Finally, after nearly tripping over the cat for the third time, he picked it up by the scruff of its neck and carried it none too gently to the barn. The cat, of course, found its way out and was back within half an hour, without learning anything from the experience. Still, Andrew managed to finish his work by suppertime.

"If that black cat wasn't such a good mouser, I think I'd shoot it," Andrew announced unexpectedly at the supper table. "I tripped over it at least three times this afternoon."

Selina looked startled at this unexpected proclamation.

"I skinned my knuckles twice and even hit my head against the mower bar because of it!" He rubbed his head at the memory, while she chuckled at the mental picture.

She sobered quickly when she saw his determined look as he got up from the table. "I am going to at least get a start on reading that book," he said. "It has made my life miserable long enough, and I want to get it over with."

He strode into the bedroom and sat down at his desk, opening the journal to the first page.

What About the Shop?

3

I hate sleepless nights. They bring out the worst in you.
—Andrew Martin

Knock! Knock! Knock!

Andrew hadn't even had a chance to read the first sentence. *Now what? Will I never get a chance to read this journal in peace?* He strained to listen as Selina answered the door.

"Good evening. Is Andrew at home?" Andrew couldn't quite place the voice, though it sounded familiar. Reluctantly he closed the journal and pulled his desktop shut.

"Yes, he is." He heard Selina reply. "Why don't you come in and have a seat while I call him?"

Andrew recognized Peter as soon as he saw him. *Of course—I should have known that voice.* He took a chair across the table from Peter, a single man in his upper twenties, who lived with his parents a mile or so down the road.

"Good evening, Peter. What brings you here tonight?" Andrew

asked. He glanced at Selina. "Could you make us some tea?"

Selina had returned to her dish washing, but she nodded. "I just put the water on. It should be ready soon." She moved over to the china cabinet to get some tea cups. "Do you take sugar or honey with your tea?" she asked Peter.

"Honey, please," Peter replied.

The two men made small talk about the weather and crops until they finished drinking their tea. Then Peter finally got to the point. "I was wondering what your mother was going to do with your father's shop, now that he is gone." He pulled his chair a bit closer to the table.

Andrew blinked in surprise. "We've never even talked about that," he said. "As far as I know, none of us has even been in it since he died. Why? What were you thinking?"

Peter squirmed a bit. "Well, I've always enjoyed woodworking," he admitted. "I think I'm fairly good at it, though probably not as good as your father was. I wondered if your mother would consider renting the shop and equipment to me. Or I could buy the equipment and pay her for it out of the profits. Either way, I'd try to take good care of it."

Andrew bit his lip. "Oh, I'm not worried that you wouldn't take care of it," he assured Peter. "It's just a new idea, that's all. We haven't even cleaned up the shop or decided what to do with the lumber he has got stacked in the shed."

"I could buy some of the lumber," Peter offered, fidgeting with his empty tea cup, which Selina promptly refilled. He cleared his throat and took a swallow of tea. "I've got some money put away, though not enough to buy the inventory and equipment outright.

"But my father would help me get started," he added quickly. "He helped all my brothers buy farms, and he wants to help me get going on something too. It's nice and close to our place, and I could board at home for now."

Andrew nodded. "I can see that it would work out well for you," he glanced out the window at the evening sky. "It's still early. Why don't we go over there and talk to my mother about it? If she doesn't mind, we could look at the shop as well and see how you like it.

"I'll hitch up," he added. "You can ride along with me."

As usual, Naomi met them at the door when they drove in. "Hello, Peter," she said, nodding silently to Andrew. "Come right in. What brings you here this evening?"

Andrew spoke first. "Peter's been thinking of starting a wood shop, a bit like Father had. He was wondering if you would consider renting Father's shop and equipment to him."

Peter nodded his assent to Andrew's statement. "That is, if you want to rent it out," he said anxiously. "I don't want to force you."

Naomi smiled at his anxiety, but hesitated before answering. "I have been thinking about the shop," she admitted. "I wasn't sure what to do with it. It would seem strange to have someone else working out there. But it's silly to not put it to use."

She walked to the window and stared sightlessly through the dusk toward the shop. "I don't know what to say," she finally said. "It would be nice to hear the saws and planers working again. But it wouldn't be the same."

She walked back to the table and sat down. "Give me a week to think about it."

Peter got to his feet. "That's fine," he assured her. "I'll drop by Andrew's place again in a week or two. You can tell him what you want to do."

"Did you want to look at the shop before you go?" Andrew asked.

Naomi looked startled by this suggestion. Peter noticed her reaction and quickly answered, "We don't need to do that tonight. I've been in it before and I'm sure it would be fine for what I want." He headed for the door, and then stopped as Andrew started getting up to follow. "Don't get up," he said. "I'll just walk home. It isn't that far."

Naomi walked back to the window and watched him go. "He's a nice young man," she mused. "It's not that I have anything against him renting it. In fact, I'd rather have him here than some older man, closer to my age."

She sighed and returned to her chair at the table. "But I just don't know what to say, I guess. I have so many memories of your father and that shop. He set it up before we were married, and it's always been part of our marriage."

"You don't need to decide tonight," Andrew said soothingly. "And we won't force you to rent it out unless you want to. There is plenty of time for that. And you don't need the money."

He leaned back in his chair and stared at the ceiling. His earlier determination to read the journal had vanished. "Why don't we walk out to the shop and look around," he suggested. "Has anyone been in it since Father died?"

Naomi shook her head. "I didn't have the courage to go out there alone," she replied. "Let's go out before you go home. If you have time, that is," she added.

It was a strange feeling for both of them to walk into the shop. Andrew stopped inside the door and looked around. Not much had changed since the days he had helped his father put together buggy boxes in the back of the shop. Buggy boxes, kitchen cabinets, wardrobes, along with dining room tables and chairs, and the occasional coffin, had kept Sylvester busy. He had brought in a good income from this shop.

He glanced up at the line shaft that powered the equipment, vaguely noticing that the belt driving a large table saw had slipped from its pulley. Even the line shaft brought back old memories. When he was a seventeen-year-old, he had helped his father remove the old water wheel that was previously the power source for the shop. They had replaced it with a stationary Heald steam engine that Sylvester had bought at an auction in the city.

"I suppose that steam engine is still working okay?" He looked at his mother.

She nodded. "He just told me about a month ago that it was the best investment he ever made. The water wheel simply wasn't able to provide enough momentum, and too often his equipment would stall while he was working."

"Evidently, he didn't get a chance to sweep up before he left for town that night," Andrew commented, kicking a wood sliver out of his way. "He used to clean up his shop every night. He was a very organized person."

"That was one of his strong points," Naomi agreed. "Always, every night, he swept up and put all his tools away. He never lost anything."

"Did he have any projects he was working on?" Andrew asked idly. "I don't see anything partly finished in the shop." His eyes traveled the length of the shop and halted. "What's that package sitting on his desk back there?"

He walked to the back of the shop and picked up the parcel curiously. "It's addressed to him, but there's no postage. Someone local must have given it to him."

Andrew examined the parcel a little more closely and saw that someone had already opened it. "Either this is a used box, or he already opened it," he said. "I'm going to see what it is."

He opened the box, which proved to be empty except for some crumpled packing paper and a scrap of paper with some writing on it. "Hmm, what's this?" He spoke half to himself as he picked up the note and read it out loud.

Hi Sylvester,
Here's the "gift" I promised you.
See you soon.
S.M.

He met his mother's eyes and saw his own questions reflected in them.

It was almost dark by the time Andrew got home that evening. Selina was watching anxiously for him at the window when he drove in. He went straight to the barn with his horse.

"So, is Peter going to rent the shop?" she asked when Andrew finally came in from the barn. "It sure took you a while."

Andrew sank onto a chair by the table, his teeth worrying his lip. "What a day," he shook his head. "You won't believe what I found in Father's shop."

Selina's eyes widened. "Another journal," she guessed.

Andrew exhaled harshly. "One journal is enough," he said. "Mother and I went out to look at the shop after Peter left. She is probably going to rent the shop to him, but she will let him know in the next week or two.

"Anyway, we went out to have a look around since no one has been in it since Father died." He stretched and yawned. "My, I'm tired tonight. Maybe I'll be able to sleep for a change."

Selina waited for him to continue with his story. "Anyhow, he must have been intending to clean up the shop when he got home from town. It was in quite a mess, which is unusual for him. I found a box on his shop desk. It just had some packing paper in it and this note." He dug the scrap of paper from his shirt pocket. "I'm not sure what this means. Evidently, someone had given him something, but Mother has no idea what it would have been. She couldn't think of anyone whose name starts with S; not anyone he would have been getting something from anyway." Andrew fell silent.

"Do you think that's why he was in town that evening?" Selina asked. She was still examining the paper. "This handwriting is pretty neat for a man. Do you suppose it could have been from a woman?"

Andrew looked startled. "I never thought of that," he admitted. "But you're right, it does look like a woman's handwriting." He pursed his lips, and his teeth found his lip again. "It's too late now, but I *am* going to start reading that journal tomorrow. Something is fishy here, and I want to know what it is."

Andrew didn't sleep well that night. And because of that Selina didn't either. Normally she was out of bed with a bounce, ready for a new day. This morning she sat on the side of the bed, rubbing her eyes. "Oh my, but I'm tired!" She yawned, desperately wishing she could just crawl back in.

Andrew didn't look much better than Selina did. He stumbled over a boot he had left in the middle of the bedroom floor and slipped on the hooked rug, almost landing on his rear before regaining his balance. He didn't swear, but the growl he let slip was the next thing to it. Despite herself, Selina giggled behind him.

"At least you can't blame it on the cat this time."

Andrew rolled his eyes. "It was my fault," he admitted. "I didn't put my boots away last night. My father must have given me a hundred lectures on putting my things away, while I was growing up. He would never have left his boots in the middle of the floor." He shook his head, and then chuckled. "I almost landed on my rear that time. This hooked rug is sure slippery on the hardwood floor. That would have been quite a sight."

Selina giggled again. "It actually was quite a sight, the way you danced around on one leg. You should be a dancer!"

Andrew made a face, but otherwise ignored her comment, which brought another giggle from Selina.

He sat on the chair by his desk and started lacing his boots, changing the subject. "Sounds like it's raining out there. Good thing I didn't mow the hay field yesterday." A rumble of thunder echoed from the hills across the fields behind the house, as if in agreement with his words.

"I need some coffee this morning," Andrew said as he opened the bedroom door. "I'll stir up the fire and get some water boiling while you get dressed."

Selina joined Andrew in the kitchen a few minutes later, and stood at the sink to run a comb through her hair.[1] "Pour me a cup of coffee too, please," she said, pulling her head covering into place and tying the ribbons under her chin. "You really tossed and turned last night." Selina's concerned glance touched her husband as she sat down at the table. "Was something troubling you?"

Andrew let her question hang while he took a drink of black coffee. "Ah! That sure hits the spot," he said. "I needed something to wake me up." He got up and walked over to the stove for some more hot water to make another cup of coffee.

He carried his cup to the window and watched the rain for a few moments. Finally, he returned to her earlier question. "I just couldn't sleep last night. This whole thing is starting to get under my skin." He set his cup on the windowsill and shoved his hands into his pockets, a picture of utter dejection.

Selina joined him at the window, slipping her arm around his waist. "You mean the journal and the note?"

He shrugged. "I've always had a real struggle with my father," he admitted. "My childhood and teen years kept going through my mind all night. He wasn't very easy to get along with. Even my mother walked on eggs when he was in a bad mood. And now, to top it all off, he goes and leaves behind a situation like this."

He pulled Selina close. "God forbid that I should ever do something like that to you." Selina was surprised to see tears in his eyes. "It just isn't right."

Finally, he turned toward the door with a sigh. "I'll do the chores while you make breakfast. I want to work on reading that journal after breakfast. It's raining anyway, so there won't be any outside

---

[1] Bathrooms were unheard of in these times, especially in rural properties.

work today." The tightly-wound spring pulled the screen door shut with a bang behind him.

Selina watched through the window for a moment as he trudged toward the barn. She could see the discouraged sag in his shoulders, even from where she stood.

A Visit to the Bishop

4

It seems the sins we despise the most in other people are the ones quickest to take root in our own lives. So, we'd best be careful about condemning others too quickly . . .
—Selina Martin

Andrew was especially quiet during breakfast. Selina tried several times to start up a conversation before lapsing into a compassionate silence. But it seemed as if Andrew came to some sort of a decision while he ate. He finished his plate of scrambled eggs and fried potatoes, then pushed it back and poured another cup of coffee. He leaned back in his chair, more relaxed than he had been all morning.

"I'm going over to talk to Bishop George," he announced. "It's raining, and he won't be working in the fields today, so maybe he'll have time to talk."

He took a sip of hot coffee and grimaced. "Whew, that's hot!" he said. "Now I've burned my tongue for the day." He blew on his coffee to cool it a few degrees. Now that he had made up his mind, he seemed anxious to get going.

It relieved Selina to have her Andrew back, rather than the stranger who had sat at the table eating in glum silence. "Did you discover something else you wanted to tell him?" she asked, curious.

"No, not really," Andrew replied. "But I've got to get rid of this bitterness toward my father. And I think maybe it would help to share my feelings with the bishop." He finished his coffee, and slid his chair back from the table. "I hate to dump more on him," he acknowledged. "But going through that journal might be easier if I can get this . . . this . . ." he paused, groping for the right word, "if I can get this cancer out of my system.

"Thanks for the good breakfast." He bent to give her a quick hug.

Selina smiled. "Now you run along," she said, pretending to give him a push toward the door. "And make sure you're smiling again when you come back." He managed a slight smile and walked out the door. She watched him from the window for the second time that morning, and couldn't help noting the difference in his stride. *I hope his visit with the bishop helps as much as he expects it to*, she mused. *He's been getting pretty depressed.*

Bishop George came from the barn as Andrew drove in the lane. He greeted Andrew cheerily. "So how are you this fine, wet morning?" Andrew returned his greeting, and pulled his horse to a stop by the hitching post.

The bishop waved him toward the driving shed. "Pull your horse and buggy inside," he offered. "It's too wet to just leave your horse tied outside. Amos won't mind." The bishop and his wife lived in a small apartment attached to the end of the main house, where their son, Amos, lived with his wife and family. Their son had run the farm for a number of years, though George still helped with the work when he had time.

Andrew followed the bishop into the apartment, wiping his feet carefully on the mat at the door.

The bishop had guessed that Andrew had something on his mind, and led the way into the parlor, carefully closing the door behind them for privacy. "So, what brings you out on such a wet morning?" he asked Andrew after they had both settled into comfortable chairs.

Andrew bit his lip, smiled sheepishly at the involuntary action, and then did it again. "I've been struggling since my father died," he said. "We never got along well while I was at home, and it's been bothering me."

He shifted uneasily in his chair. "I had sort of put it behind me since I got married, but standing beside his coffin, it all came flooding back. And now with what I've learned about his business practices, and the journal, I almost can't handle it anymore."

He looked desperately at the bishop. "I want to get rid of this weight before it destroys me. And I don't know what to do about it."

Bishop George nodded. "Why don't you tell me about it?" he invited. "Sometimes it helps to talk about our troubles."

"Well, I don't think I ever could do things right for my father," Andrew began. "Even before I started school, I knew that." He stared at the ceiling as memories came flooding back, and he shared them briefly with Bishop George . . .

"Andrew!" The little boy jumped—startled, though not surprised—at the bark of his father's voice. "You didn't shut the barn door." Six-year-old Andrew cringed, remembering too late that he had been told to make sure he always closed the door when he went to the house.

"You go out there right now and close it, then take what you've got coming!" Andrew's teeth almost chattered at the stern words. It was dark and cold outside, and the wind howled eerily around the house. Like most young children, he was afraid of the dark. But he was also afraid of his father. His father didn't give him a chance to decide what to do, but marched him to the door.

Andrew survived the trip, and what followed, but it took him days to forget.

Things hadn't changed much by the time he was ten . . .

Andrew's cousin was visiting during those summer holidays, which made the humiliation worse.

"Andrew!" He jumped, wondering what was wrong. Sylvester's voice was a harsh growl. "Finish eating your meat. Don't push what you don't want behind your plate."

Andrew stared at the table. The "meat" his father was referring to was a small pile of tendons which Andrew had tried to chew but couldn't. He started to open his mouth to protest, but the scowl on his father's face stopped him.

Naomi spoke up this time. "Surely he doesn't have to eat the tendons," she said timidly. The expression on Sylvester's face stopped her, too.

"He needs to learn to finish what he takes," Sylvester told her coldly. The threatening look on his face implied that she needed to learn to stay out of it when he disciplined his son.

Andrew's cousin looked on with his mouth open, then quickly checked to make sure he had cleaned his own plate to his uncle's specifications. This was a completely new kind of home life for him.

Andrew managed to swallow his "meat" though he gagged a few times before he succeeded. The two boys left the table hurriedly, heading outside as soon as they were allowed to go. Embarrassed tears streamed down Andrew's face. "It was just a pile of tendons," he told his cousin resentfully. "He himself would never eat them."

And not even by the time he was in his upper teens . . .

"Andrew!" The boy still jumped at the severity in his father's voice, although he was eighteen now. "Were you using my hammer and awl? They aren't on the workbench where they belong!"

Andrew's mind raced in panic. Where had he seen those tools? Surely they weren't still out in the driving shed where he had fixed that piece of harness yesterday. He stuttered as he answered, "I . . .

um, I was using them to fix a harness yesterday in the driving shed. I . . . I thought I put them away, but . . ." He stopped at the look on his father's face.

"Go and get them right now," his father snapped.

Andrew raced for the driving shed, hoping that the hammer and awl actually were there.

They were. He breathed a sigh of relief, trying to calm his racing heartbeat. Disaster had been averted once again.

"I know I tended to be a bit careless at times," Andrew said now, bitterly. "But somehow, no matter how hard I tried, I would forget to put something away, or to close the barn door, or whatever. It seemed that he picked on everything I did wrong and never noticed anything I did right."

The bishop nodded his head sympathetically. "I'm not surprised. Sylvester was a hard man." He paused. "Did things get better when you got married?"

Andrew scuffed his shoe against the floor.

"It went some better after we were married," he answered wearily. "But that was mostly because I wasn't around him as much. We didn't go home a lot—not as much as we probably should have, for my mother's sake. Gradually, though, I learned to forget most of the worst memories.

"But when I stood beside his coffin, it all came flooding back. I sure hope I can be the kind of father and husband that will leave my family with fonder memories when I'm in my coffin." He drew a deep breath. "I feel horrible for having such an attitude. He was my father, after all. I should be missing him, rather than thinking bitter thoughts.

"And now, with finding this journal and hearing about his shady business practices, I could really hate him. He has put our whole family in an upheaval." Andrew came to an abrupt stop, looking at Bishop George beseechingly. "I know it isn't right, but I can't help myself."

The bishop waited a few moments before answering. "It's a hard thing, and it can take some time," he replied thoughtfully. "We don't preach a lot about home relationships in our churches, and I know of people who would have applauded your father for his actions in each of your examples. It is possible that you will be grateful one day for some of his training, even if he gave it in a wrong way. However, I am concerned about the harsh attitudes that so many fathers in our churches have, and especially about the lack of good relationships with their children. We have too many young men and women leaving our churches and going to the Methodists, and I think this lack of relationship is part of the problem.

"I'm not sure I have any easy answers for your dilemma, Andrew. Time should heal some of your feelings. But I think it is important for you to forgive. Judgment belongs to God, not to us. Ask God for grace to forgive your father. Think of the good he did and remember those things."

Bishop George hesitated and looked keenly at the young man before him. "Do you read the Bible on a personal or a family level?" he asked. "I know that some people frown on this, but I believe God speaks to us through the Bible about many such problems."

Andrew looked a little surprised. "Not a lot, really," he admitted. "My father used to say we should leave that to the preachers and that Bible thumpers are just proud people who want to be ordained. I could probably count on the fingers of one hand the number of times I saw him reading the Bible."

The bishop stroked his beard. "Right there, I'm afraid, is part of the reason for your father's problems. I know his sentiments are common—too common—but I hope the church will gradually come to realize the fallacy of such ideas. I realize not many agree with me, but I believe that will change in time. The Bible says we will be blessed if we hunger and thirst after righteousness, and the best place to find instruction on righteousness is in the Bible."

Andrew nodded. "I can see that," he replied. "But I find it hard to read German. My education was all in English. Selina probably reads the Bible more than I do, but she says the same thing."

Bishop George lowered his voice. "If that is the case, why not buy an English Bible? I have a copy of the King James Version that I use in studying, and I find it very helpful at times."

"Really?" Andrew looked as startled as he sounded. "I thought it was wrong to read the Bible in English." He looked confused. "I brought an English New Testament home from school one time and my father burned it. He said God doesn't speak the devil's language."

It was the bishop's turn to look surprised. "Well, I knew Sylvester was conservative, but I didn't know he held *that* strongly to his ideas."

He tugged at his beard. "I'm a little careful about recommending an English Bible, since some of our people would feel as your father did. But I do think some of the weaknesses in our churches could be helped if people read the Bible more—and in a language they understand."

Andrew nodded. "I'll get one. Selina will like that. She's an avid reader, but she finds it more difficult in German."

"As far as your feelings about your father," the bishop continued, "I think you do need to forgive him for his failures toward you and your family. The Bible talks about the damage that comes from 'a root of bitterness.' Try to remember that he was human, just as you are, and try to give him the same benefit of the doubt that you would want from others. Make deliberate efforts to remember his good points when you are tempted to think about his bad points.

"As I said, it will take time. But I think as you continue to pray about it, and concentrate on loving the people around you, things will gradually go better."

Andrew had a lot to think about as he drove home. *I should have gone to see Bishop George before. It helped just to talk about my problem. But I'm surprised that he would recommend an English Bible. None of the ministers has ever said anything like that in a sermon, at least not that I can remember.*

When he drove in at home, he was surprised to see a horse and buggy tied at the hitching post. *Why, that's Dad's buggy,* he thought. *Why would Mother be here to see us? She must have hitched up all by herself.*

Worried, he pulled his horse and buggy up beside his mother's and tied his horse there instead of unhitching. He hurried into the house.

Naomi Has an Unexpected Visitor

5

Sometimes I wonder just how many more secrets will come to light.
—Naomi Martin

It was easy for Andrew to see that something had agitated his mother. She jumped to her feet as he removed his shoes and left them on the mat.

"I'm so glad you're home," Naomi exclaimed. "The strangest thing happened this morning, and I thought I should talk to you about it.

"I was just finishing my breakfast when a stranger on horseback rode into the lane," she continued. "He looked scruffy, with a straggly beard and a battered cowboy hat. He tied his horse to the fence and stomped up the porch steps. Here's what happened."

"I hear that old Sylvester done kicked the bucket," the stranger drawled.

Naomi was too taken aback to reply to this abrupt announcement, but she nodded.

"Well, Sylvester used to play cards with me, and he done ran up quite a list of losses. He promised he'd pay me at the end of the month."

The stranger seemed to recall at this moment that he was addressing a lady, and a recently widowed lady at that, and he pulled off his hat. "Well, I don't have any call to make anyone's lot any harder for them," he said apologetically. "What with you being left on your own so sudden-like. And I suspect old Sylvester wasn't all that easy to live with for a God-fearing lady like yourself." His eyes lingered on Naomi's head covering.

He caught himself again. "Well, as I said, I don't got no call to make life harder for a widow-lady, but I'm a poor man, you see. Winnings have been slim since Sylvester stopped dropping by the saloon to play, so I thought I'd drop by a list of his losses and see if you could come up with some cash for me." The stranger handed her a paper.

Naomi's head spun. She automatically glanced at the paper in her hand. She didn't take it all in, but she did see the total: $275. She caught her breath, her hand going to her heart.

"Oh my." Her voice trembled. "I don't have anywhere near that much money here at home, and my son takes care of my financial affairs since Sylvester died. I . . . I'll have to speak to him about it."

The stranger seemed disappointed but not surprised. "Well, you talk to him, and see what you can do." He squirmed a bit. "Like I said, I don't have any call to make life hard for you, but I'm needing the money terrible bad. If your boy could drop by the saloon in town in the next day or so with the money, I'd be mighty grateful. Tell him to ask for Wes."

He rubbed the toe of his riding boot on the porch, and his eyes narrowed. "It wouldn't be a good idea for him to make a problem for me. I make my livin' playing cards, but I'm not a shark. I play tough, but I play honest, and I expect others to be honest as well."

*With this veiled threat, he turned and stomped his way back
to his horse, replacing his hat as he went.*

"He didn't look like the kind of person to mess with," Naomi concluded nervously. "Oh, dear. I had no idea that Sylvester had gotten
into gambling! How do we know if this man's demand is legitimate?
He kept saying that he didn't want to make life hard for me, but I'm
not sure what he would do if we refused him."

Andrew's brows rose as he studied the losses totaled on the paper.
"Why would Father have done such a thing?" He was dumbfounded.
"Going into a saloon, associating with drunkards and gamblers, wast-
ing all that time and money . . ." Andrew slowly shook his head in
bewilderment. "And it's not as though he needed more money."

Naomi looked as baffled as Andrew felt. "Maybe that's what he
was doing those nights when he was gone late. He always said he
was meeting a customer, but I often wondered about it." She hesitated before adding softly, almost as if she were speaking to herself,
"Well, maybe I should be glad that is all it was."

Andrew glanced at Selina, but didn't follow up on his mother's
involuntary comment. However, he could see that Selina had noticed
it too. After a moment of silence, he sighed heavily.

"Well, I suppose I might as well go to the bank and get him his
money. Hopefully that will satisfy him and won't bring the rest of
the town's gamblers to the door with similar claims," Andrew said
bitterly.

He walked to the window and stared out. "It doesn't look like this
rain is going to let up. Why don't we have a bite to eat before you
go home, and I'll drive into town and get his money. What did you
say his name was?"

Andrew had a lot to think about on his way to town. So, another
unpleasant surprise. *I guess we had better be prepared for anything, the*

way it seems. He remembered the bishop's words. *I need to forgive him for this too. This one is not going to be easy. If Father had caught me gambling, he would have given me a strapping that left me black and blue for a week.* He fought feelings of betrayal.

The crumpled slip of paper listed the gambler's winnings from Sylvester. Each figure was dated. If the gambler was to be trusted, Sylvester had been playing cards at least once a week for some time. *I wonder if he ever won? Or why he kept on playing if he always lost? I might need to have a bit of a chat with this Wes character.*

For the first time in his life, Andrew stepped into the local saloon. He stopped inside the door to let his eyes adjust to the gloomy interior. Apparently, it wasn't a busy time of day because only a few people were sitting at tables and at the bar itself. In a corner, several hard-looking men were playing cards, and Andrew wondered if one of them was Wes. An uncomfortable prickle started at the back of his neck as he walked up to the bar.

"Is Wes here?" he asked the bartender, overriding the gruff, "What'll you have?"

The bartender looked surprised, and he eyed Andrew up and down. He opened his mouth to comment, then changed his mind and gestured toward the back corner at the men Andrew had already noticed. "Back there." Then he added guardedly, "You're not one of his regulars."

"I've never met him," Andrew answered, "but I understand that my father knew him."

The bartender's eyes widened. "Ah, you're Sylvester's son, are you?" It wasn't really a question, and the bartender didn't wait for an answer. "Wes said Sylvester died and left him stuck with his losses. So, Wes was out to see you, was he?"

This time the question was real. Andrew wasn't sure why it was any of the bartender's business, but he answered anyway.

"No, but he stopped to see my mother." He shifted uneasily under the bartender's penetrating glance. "My mother pays her bills, and if my father owed Wes money, she'll pay him. But I'm hoping that will be the end of it," he finished firmly.

"You'll need to sort that out with Wes," the bartender replied. He lowered his voice a bit and glanced toward the back corner where the two card players had finished their game and were leaning back in their chairs. "Go easy with him though. He isn't the kind of person who takes kindly to people pushing him around. My advice is, pay up and leave him be. You don't want to irritate him."

Andrew hesitated and then spoke, more quietly. "I guess I'm curious how my father got involved with him. Father wasn't the kind who would keep on playing a losing game."

A curious look flickered across the bartender's face. "Well," he said knowingly, "Sylvester used to stop in here fairly regular for a glass to wet his whistle. Never drank much, mind you, but we all got to know him, and Wes was teaching him how to play cards. After a while, they got to playing for real, and then Wes started pressuring him to pay up. Threatened to visit Sylvester's bishop and tell him what all was going on during Sylvester's visits to town. They had quite a ruckus the last time Sylvester was here; one was as stubborn as the other, and both liked their dollars. But Sylvester didn't want Wes to talk to the wrong people, so he promised he'd pay."

Clearly, the bartender was thinking of commenting further, but changed his mind. "Go talk to Wes," he said abruptly. "If you got any more questions, ask him. Just don't make him mad. It isn't worth it." The bartender moved off to draw a drink for a customer beckoning impatiently from the other end of the bar.

Andrew watched him go, then turned on his heel and walked to the card table. Neither of the men returned his greeting, but the shiftier looking of the two grunted when Andrew asked, "One of you fellows named Wes?"

Andrew pulled up a chair and sat down, tugging an envelope of cash from his pocket and laying it on the table. "My mother wanted me to give you this," he said. "Apparently my father owed you some money?"

The gambler snatched up the envelope and counted the money.

"Looks okay," he said. "Anything else on your mind?" he added when Andrew made no move to leave. His eyes narrowed as he met Andrew's gaze. "Not thinking of raising a fuss, now, are you? I won that money fair and square. Sylvester wasn't the world's best card player." A rusty chuckle ground out of his throat.

Andrew's gaze didn't shift; eventually the tough gambler was the first to drop his eyes. "I'm not raising a fuss," Andrew answered quietly. "My father made his own decisions, and I'm not here to defend them. But I was curious if you have any more information about my father that I should know."

Andrew's bluntness seemed to startle the gambler. He glanced at his partner across the table.

The other man snickered. "Here's your chance, Wes," he drawled. "You always said you were going to bust old Sylvester's life wide open some day."

Wes wavered a bit. "Look, son," he said. "There's probably some things you'll be happier not knowing. You look like you take after your mother in her religious beliefs, and there's some things that you wouldn't understand about your father. I've got my money, and I got no call to bad-mouth Sylvester, or cause your mother more grief. I'm sure she's had her share, knowing your old man. You just follow her trail in life and you won't have to worry about dealing with guys like me."

"Anyway," Wes added curtly, "I've got some customers coming through the door right soon."

Andrew took the hint and got to his feet.

Wes watched him go, a curious look on his face. "You know," he said to his partner, "if I'd had a mother like his, I might be different."

His partner snorted. "Fat chance of that. You're bad to the core. God sure wouldn't have anything to do with the likes of you." He picked up the pack of cards and started to deal them.

Wes picked up his hand of cards and didn't say anything more. But a wistful look crossed his face as they started to play.

Andrew was already out of town when he remembered his plan to buy an English Bible. He wheeled his horse and buggy around and headed back to the small book store on Main Street. He browsed through the display of Bibles for a bit before choosing a medium-priced, leather bound Bible printed in easy-to-read type. It was a bit more money than he had expected to spend, but he expected it would get lots of use, and he decided it was worth the money.

He was still uneasy about buying an English Bible, and he glanced up and down the street as he left the store. *Hopefully no one from church saw me come out with an English Bible under my arm. I'm pretty sure lots of people would disagree with the bishop on this one.*

Andrew laid his parcel carefully on the buggy seat before untying Duke. He glanced at the saloon as he drove by, but didn't see anyone he knew. *The windows are all darkened and you can't see inside. Father could have been in there without worrying about being seen, unless someone familiar stopped in for a glass of cider. But he usually came to town late in the day when most of our people were doing chores and eating supper. He was fairly safe from exposure, I guess.*

He picked up the parcel from the seat and undid the brown paper wrapping. Duke knew the way home, and was anxious to get there for his own supper. He needed little urging or guiding. This left Andrew free to explore the new Bible. Since all the preaching and Bible reading he had ever heard were in German, he still felt quivery at the idea of reading a Bible translated into English.[1] He knew all too well how his father felt about the idea.

Andrew left the Bible on the buggy seat while he did his chores. When he entered the kitchen, Selina had supper on the table.

"Did you get that gambler paid up and satisfied?" she asked

---

[1] This was to become a major issue in the Mennonite Church within the next several decades, and Andrew would live to see the time that the church divided over the issues of language, Sunday School, and evening services.

curiously. "Your mother was pretty worried about it all."

"I stopped in to tell her I was okay," Andrew said. "It wasn't that bad really. But I asked the gambler about Father and he wouldn't tell me anything. He said I'm better off not knowing, and that he didn't want to make Mother's load heavier for her. I was surprised how concerned he seemed to be about her, a tough fellow like that.

"I talked a bit to the bartender, and he warned me not to push Wes too hard," he added. "I think he's got a reputation in town for being a tough guy. But I didn't have any trouble with him." Then he lay his package on the table.

Selina's eyes widened when she saw the Bible. "An English Bible," she gasped. "Are we allowed to have them?"

"Bishop George suggested I get one," Andrew reassured her. "He's not against them, though I'm sure lots of other people are. Let's see what it's like."

They spent the evening with the Bible, marveling at how clear it seemed in English. Selina put it into words for both of them as they got ready for bed. "It's like getting a message from heaven. We need to spend more time reading together."

Andrew agreed. "It would be good for both of us." He walked past his desk and noticed the journal. "Oh, dear. I forgot all about that journal. It's too late now. I'll have to look at it tomorrow."

"Tomorrow is church," Selina reminded him. "We'll probably have company."

He nodded. "That's right, I forgot it's our Sunday to have church. But I am about ready to stop delaying it!"

Sunday 6

For where two or three are gathered together in my name,
there am I in the midst of them.
—Jesus

Andrew was up early the next morning so that he could finish his chores and get to church on time. They had several churches within driving distance, each of which had services every other week on alternate Sundays. Each of the local Mennonite families considered one of the two churches to be their home church, but most attended Sunday morning services regularly at both churches. At this time in history, most Mennonite churches didn't have evening or weekday services. It was normal either to visit another family for Sunday dinner after church,[1] or to have someone visit you. The home church people expected company when their church had services, but they seldom knew who would show up, since invitations

---

[1] Most people had chores to do and went home for supper. The youth would gather after supper at a home for a "singing" which afterward often included games of various sorts.

normally were not expected or given. If you were a visitor, you were expected to choose a place to go for dinner. It was considered good manners to try to visit everyone in the congregation, not just your close friends.

This Sunday Andrew and Selina's congregation was hosting services, so Selina was busy getting ready for company while Andrew did his chores. He finished these in record time and was back in the house before Selina had breakfast quite ready.

"Could you get some butter from the ice house and put it in the dumbwaiter to soften?" The dumbwaiter, a small pantry-like elevator with shelves, allowed food to be lowered to the cool basement or raised to the warmer kitchen as needed, using pulleys and weights for easy movement. Selina continued scrubbing and peeling potatoes. She put them in a crock of cold water and covered them with a cloth before adding them to the dumbwaiter. The first person home from church, even if it was a visitor, would slice the potatoes and put them on the stove to cook. The meal, which was simple yet tasty, consisted of sliced potatoes boiled in water served with cream and sliced meat, such as summer sausage. As was typical, Selina added bread and jam, various pickles, and a vegetable that was in season.

"What are you serving for dessert?" Andrew peered into a dish.

"I made some apple pies from the windfalls of the old apple tree behind the house," she replied. "They won't keep for winter anyway, and we'll have lots of apples this year."

Andrew nodded, then glanced at the new Bible lying on the corner cabinet. "Do we have time for Bible reading this morning?"

"Let's take time," said Selina. "Anyway, I'm about ready."

Andrew turned to Ephesians, a book that had caught his eye the evening before, and started reading at the beginning. "Paul, an apostle of Jesus Christ by the will of God, to the saints which are at Ephesus, and to the faithful in Christ Jesus," he began. He looked over at Selina and seeing that she was listening intently, he continued.

After reading several more verses, he paused and glanced at the old kitchen clock. "I guess I'd better stop there for this morning." He gently closed the Bible. "Verse five says God chose us before the creation of the world," he mused. He looked at Selina. "Do you think that means God knew we were going to be born someday, way back then before He created the world? And that we would follow Him?"

Selina's face lit up. "That's what it says," she confirmed. "That's a wonderful thought. I like that idea."

Andrew bit his lip thoughtfully and walked across the room to pick up his German Bible. "I wonder what it says in German. I don't remember reading that before."

He flipped the pages to the passage he was looking for and read it. "Hmm. I guess it could be understood that way in German too. It uses the word *erwählt*, which certainly carries the idea of being chosen. Strange I never thought of it that way before—chosen. I always thought it meant God called everyone, but this makes it sound much more personal."

"That's what I like about it," Selina said softly. "It's personal. He saw *me* and He wanted *me*."

Andrew hesitated and then closed the Bible without further comment. He had known for a long time that Selina's faith was deeper than his. *I wonder where she gets it. My mother is like that too. Is it because they are both women?* Somehow, he didn't think that was really the reason.

The couple bowed their heads in the usual silent prayer.[2]

It took about twenty minutes for Andrew and Selina to get to church. He pulled in at the end of the line of buggies already by the side door of the church, where the women, girls, and younger

---

[2] Audible prayer was for ordained leaders only, and even a minister would not normally have prayed audibly before a meal.

children were being dropped off. The men and boys used separate doorways at the other end of the building, after they had tied up their horses.

Preacher Daniel preached the main sermon that morning. This brought back some painful memories for Andrew, as he hadn't seen Daniel since he had preached Sylvester's funeral sermon.

Daniel also remembered the funeral, and referred to it in his opening remarks. "It has now been more than a week since we laid our beloved brother, Sylvester, to rest," he began, somewhat pompously. "It behooves us to remember this as we gather this morning—any one of us could be the next person called to leave behind our earthly pursuits."

His sing-song voice droned on for more than an hour, and Andrew's mind drifted. He had come to church with an unusual feeling of anticipation, and a strong sense of desiring something, though he wasn't sure what it was. But Preacher Daniel's opening remarks had deflated him. *My father's last action on earth was cursing Daniel to his face, and now Daniel calls him a beloved brother.* Andrew subconsciously shook his head. Then he caught Bishop George eyeing him. Apparently, the bishop was wondering how he was handling the minister's words.

A change in the tone of Daniel's voice finally caught Andrew's attention. "We need to maintain the traditions of our fathers. It is easy to allow English preaching and Sunday Schools to attract us, but these worldly deviations will never bring us closer to God. The German language was good enough for our forefathers and it is good enough for us."

This time it was Andrew's turn to eye Bishop George, and he thought he caught a slight twitch of his eyebrows. *Hmm, I wonder if the Apostle Paul spoke German, or wrote in German?* He pushed the thought aside and turned his mind back to the sermon.

With Daniel's remarks still ringing in their ears, the congregation knelt again in prayer.

Andrew and Selina did have company, just as they expected. Dinner went well, and so did the afternoon discussions, spiced with a snack of well-salted popcorn and fresh apples. Andrew hurried through his evening chores, then he and Selina shared a leisurely supper of left-over potato slices and salami.

Andrew leaned back in his chair and stretched his arms toward the ceiling. "Well, that was a decent day, in spite of the sermon this morning," he yawned. "I'm tired tonight. Too much sitting around and eating."

Selina got up and started clearing the table. "So, are you going to look at the journal tonight?" she asked. "Or can we do something else?"

Andrew glanced at her. "What do you have in mind?" he asked. "Do you want to play a game of chess?"

Selina grimaced, then laughed. "No, I don't think so," she answered. "I still remember the last time we tried that. You beat me in six or seven moves."

Andrew grinned. "It was five, I think." He got to his feet and picked up his dirty plate to carry to the sink. "You need a little more practice."

"No, thanks," Selina replied firmly. "I'd rather go for a walk or drive over to visit your mother. I wonder if she had company today."

Andrew grabbed his hat from the hook by the door. "Okay, I'll go hitch up," he said. "Why don't you just stack the dishes for now, and I'll help you do them when we come home."

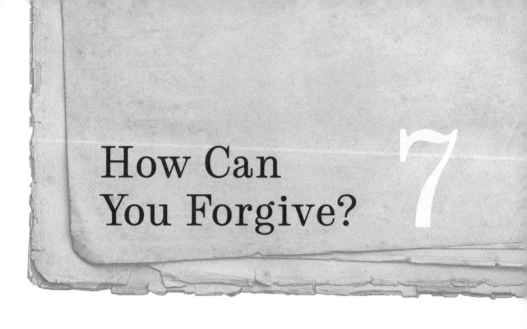

How Can You Forgive?

7

How oft shall my brother sin against me,
and I forgive him? till seven times?
—Peter

Naomi was sitting on the porch, enjoying the evening breeze, when Andrew and Selina drove into her lane. "It's a beautiful evening," she greeted them. "The house was so hot, I thought I would sit outside for a while until it cools down."

"I'll get a few more chairs and we'll join you," Andrew said. "We might as well enjoy the nice weather while it lasts." He dropped his straw hat on the porch floor and entered the house. The screen door banged shut behind him.

Selina pulled off her bonnet, and let the evening breezes play through her blond hair. "It's such a beautiful evening," she said to her mother-in-law. "I just couldn't bear the idea of sitting in the house with nothing interesting to do until bed time."

Andrew came back out the door with two chairs, in time to hear this remark. He grinned playfully. "I did offer to play chess with you," he said, pretending to be offended. "But you didn't want to."

Selina stuck out her tongue at him. "I said I wanted something *interesting* to do," she retorted. "I don't consider being beaten at chess three games in a row to be interesting."

Andrew chuckled, and set a chair for her beside his mother's. He put his own chair on the other side of Selina's and sat down, one leg crossing the other as he relaxed.

Selina sat down primly beside him, and then relented. "Well, I'd rather play chess with you than anything else with someone else. But I think fig mill[1] would be more down my line."

Naomi started to get up. "Did you want to play? I've got a fig mill game," she said, speaking of the board game that was popular in the community.

Selina quickly stopped her. "No, no," she protested. "I was just 'funning'. Let's just sit here and talk. You must get lonesome, being here alone all the time."

Naomi smiled and sat down again. "Well, it gets a bit lonely sometimes, with the girls away on their jobs as maids," she admitted. "But people drop by occasionally, and I'm still doing some garden work and drying some apples for winter."

She looked wistfully across the yard to the unused shop across the way. "Truthfully, it's not that much different than it was when Sylvester was still here, except it is quieter, and I am alone for meals and sleeping."

Andrew's gaze followed hers to the silent building across the yard. "Have you thought any more about letting Peter use the shop?" He brought his gaze back to her face.

"I think I'd like for him to have it," she answered, after a pause. "He's a nice young man, and it would give him a good start. Maybe someday he could buy the place, unless one of the girls gets married to someone who wants it."

---

[1] A strategy game dating back to at least the Roman Empire, still played today in various settings.

"Maybe Peter will want one of them for a wife," Selina suggested hopefully. "He'd make a good husband, even if he is a bit shy, and short on good looks." Her smile softened the sting of her words, but Naomi remained sober.

"It's true," she answered quietly. "He isn't the best looking perhaps. And he is shy, which may explain why he never married. But I really think he would make a good husband for one of the girls." She rocked silently a few minutes before continuing soberly. "If there is one lesson I've learned in life, it is that the handsome, outgoing boys don't always make the best husbands." Her quiet voice cracked a bit.

Silence fell over the little group as her meaning sunk in. "Was that the kind of person Dad was?" Andrew asked hesitantly. "I guess I've never really heard anything about your courting days."

Naomi flushed a little under her son's steady gaze. "Half of the eligible girls in church were jealous when we started courting," she admitted. "And so were their mothers. He was considered one of the best 'catches' in church. My parents were really pleased. He was hard-working and handsome. And he was older, so he had some money saved up and an established business. Also, he was a preacher's son."

She moved her chair a few inches so she could see Andrew better. "That meant a great deal in those days, to be a preacher's son." She looked away. "I've wondered if he says anything about our courtship in his journal," she said pensively. "I was never one of the popular girls and I have often wondered why he chose me."

"I haven't read the journal yet," Andrew admitted. "Somehow, every time I think of starting it, something comes up. I think he started writing in it before you were married though. He dated all his entries, and the first one was several years before your wedding."

He stuffed his hands into his pants pockets. "I've really wondered why he kept a journal. He wasn't the literary kind as far as I can remember. I was really surprised when I found it."

"I'm not sure either why he wrote it," Naomi said. "Maybe if you read it, you will figure it out. I've been thinking of that, at times. In his own way he was a thinker, though his thinking often took a different track than other people's. He did lots of reading when he was younger, and I even saw a poem once that he had written, though he got upset when he saw me reading it. He seemed embarrassed about anything like that, almost as if things like reading and writing made him less manly.

"He told me once that if his father caught him reading, he would tell him to go and do something worthwhile," she added. "I always thought that was somewhat odd since his father was a preacher, but he was a strong believer that idleness was the devil's workshop, and viewed reading as idleness. Sylvester read the newspaper and kept up-to-date on the news. But he avoided most reading beyond that. Maybe writing in his journal met some kind of need that he had suppressed."

Naomi looked longingly across the lane at the silent shop. "There are so many things I'd like to ask him now that he is gone." She shook her head. "I was always somewhat afraid of him, but maybe if I'd tried harder, he would have softened up. I wish I could have a second chance." The confession seemed painful.

Andrew straightened in his chair. "But you were always kind to him," he protested firmly. "I remember lots of times when he was nasty to you, or to one of us children, and you always had a quiet answer for him. I don't remember you ever getting upset with him. I never could understand that."

A brief smile crossed Naomi's worn face. "I'm glad you felt that way," she said softly. "There was many a time that I went out to the garden so I could weep. I couldn't cry at night because he got upset if he saw me crying. So I had to learn to squelch my feelings."

Andrew felt the old bitterness rising within him, like a dam about to burst, and he took a deep breath. "Bishop George told me that I need to forgive Father for how he treated me, and I'm trying," he said shortly. "But I'm not sure I can ever forgive him for how he treated you." He glared at a songbird sweetly singing from its perch on a fence post at the edge of the yard.

His mother shook her head. "You never knew half of it," she said softly. "And I never had proof for some of what I think happened during those years. You might find some of that out when you read the journal. But you *must* learn to forgive. Otherwise, you will end up with a root of bitterness within you that will destroy your relationship with God and with your own family."

She wiped a tear from her cheek. "If you want to feel sorry for someone, feel sorry for your father," she said earnestly. "I have given it all to God and can think back over our married life without feeling angry. I still love Sylvester, despite everything." Her voice started to quiver. "But it's too late for him, and I'm so afraid—so afraid— that he wasn't ready to die."

Andrew was very quiet for the rest of the evening. But when they were driving home, he started to talk. He placed his arm on the back of the buggy seat and Selina slipped close to him. She had removed her bonnet, and he reached up gently to brush his hand over the soft blond hair peeking from under her head covering. But she knew his mind wasn't on her.

"How can she talk like that?" The words burst from him. "He was mean to her. Really mean! I can remember him grabbing her by the shoulders and marching her into the bedroom, and hearing her sobs. How can she say she still loves him?" He yanked viciously on the reins, then paused to calm the horse.

"And she's worrying about whether he was ready to die!" He almost shouted. "After the way he treated her . . ." He stopped when Selina stirred beside him. He thought she was going to protest or even rebuke him. But she only searched his face and remained silent. He caught her look of compassion and quieted down.

"I know it's wrong for me to feel that way." Andrew's shoulders sagged. "But every time I think I've gotten over the past, something stirs it up again."

Selina cradled his calloused hand in her soft one. "You're being too hard on yourself," she consoled him. "Your mother didn't get to where she is overnight either. It took a lot of time and a lot of prayer, I'm sure. We need to do more reading in the English Bible you bought. And more praying."

He looked doubtful. "You really think that will help?" he asked. "Preacher Daniel wouldn't be happy to hear you say that."

Her face lit up. "Yes, I believe it. God loves us, and He will show us His way."

Again, he was surprised at the assurance in her voice. "It will take a real miracle to change the way I feel," he said dubiously. "But we can try."

Selina was quiet until he stopped by the house to drop her off. "I just hope reading that journal doesn't do the wrong thing for you. Maybe we should just burn it."

Andrew's jaw clenched. "I would wonder until my dying day what was in it," he said grimly. "I might as well face up to it and get it over with. Then life can go on and things can get back to normal."

She watched him drive to the barn before she entered the dark house. "I hope so," she whispered. "I hope life will go back to normal. I don't want to lose you to bitterness."

A New Day Dawns

8

There's something about work that makes a man feel like life is
worthwhile. Most troublemakers just don't have enough to do.
—Bishop George

Monday morning dawned without a cloud. The day was
sunny and hot, but not humid—perfect haying weather. As Andrew
strode to the barn to do his chores, he felt stirring within him the
thrill that farming had always given him. For the first time since his
father's death, he looked forward to working.

"Perfect day for making hay!" The old black tomcat was the only
audience just then, but he purred his agreement and tried to rub
against Andrew's ankles. "Dumb cat," he snorted. But his response
wasn't as irritated as it would have been last week. The cat took it as
a compliment and purred even louder.

The barn was a bedlam when Andrew stepped through the door. The
pigs were the noisiest, squealing when they heard him coming. Not
once had he forgotten to feed them, but they seemed sure this would
be the first time. Each tried to outdo the other in reminding him that

yes, they were alive and yes, they were very hungry. This morning, it was music to Andrew's ears, and he grinned as he emptied the slop pail into the pig trough, watching them scramble to get the best scraps.

"Silly pigs," he laughed as he moved on to feed the other animals. "You would think they hadn't eaten for a week."

He climbed into the nearly empty haymow and threw some loose hay down the hay hole for the cattle and horses. "Good thing we've had a good hay crop this year. This mow will soon be empty." He glanced across the barn where another haymow was filled to the roof with fresh hay from his earlier cuttings. The barn's third mow was full of fresh straw. They had just finished threshing the week that Sylvester had died.

Andrew continued his one-sided conversation with himself as he went down the steps to the main part of the barn. "It'll soon be time for fall plowing, and I need to get that winter wheat planted." He still had a lot of work to do, but things were winding down already. It was a good feeling.

Right after breakfast, Andrew harnessed his team of draft horses. He was rather proud of his team, though he wouldn't have admitted it even to himself. They were one of the best teams in the area— steady workers but with enough spirit to step along with their heads held high. They could do a hard day's work and ask for more. "Those horses were the best investment I ever made," Sylvester said once. Andrew thought of that again as he led the horses out of the barn to hitch them to the mower.

Father wasn't much of a farmer, but he did have a good eye for horses, Andrew thought as he drove back the lane to the hay field at the back of his farm. He felt a twinge of guilt as he remembered his recent feelings about his father. *He bought me a pretty good farm, too.* Andrew was thankful his father had followed the usual custom of providing a farm upon his marriage, as recompense for turning his wages over to his parents up to that time. *He paid a good price for it, but it's been worth every penny.*

Andrew would always remember this Monday as the day his

struggles started to turn around for him. Maybe it had to do with the sunshine and the joy of working the land. Maybe it had to do with remembering that his father had bought him a good farm and the best team of horses in the area. But he suspected that it had just as much to do with the knowledge that Selina was praying for him as she went about her work. And, most likely, the previous night had something to do with it too.

He smiled as the memory warmed him.

> Selina sat on the side of the bed and looked at him shyly. "Do you think we could pray together before we go to bed?"
>
> It was an unusual request in their setting. Prayers were private; he could remember only two or three times in their married life that they had prayed together audibly. But he could see she was serious. He sat down on the bed beside her and took her hand. "Something troubling you?" he asked gently.
>
> Several tears ran down her cheek. "I just don't want to lose you," she said. "You've been so . . . so . . . depressed, lately."
>
> So they prayed. Andrew had thought that, after five years of marriage, he knew Selina fairly well. But he had a glimpse of her heart that night that he would never forget. They prayed together, and they cried together. Then they prayed while they cried. Then they cried and prayed and laughed. And God seemed closer that night than He had ever been. At least that was true of Andrew. He couldn't speak for Selina.

Yes, he was fairly sure that the prayers and tears he had shared with his wife last night had a lot more to do with how he felt than today's sunshine did.

It would be several days before the hay would cure enough to be hauled to the barn. In the meantime, Andrew's neighbor Josh was finishing his threshing, and since Andrew was in the same harvest group, he hurried to cut his hay so he could get there to help.

Arriving at Josh's farm, Andrew guided his team and wagon straight to the field. His wagon was the fourth one to arrive. He could see one driver unloading at the threshing machine, so he joined the others in the field.

Josh owned a reaper that had cut the grain a week earlier, but someone had to walk behind it and bind armfuls of grain into sheaves, then stook them for drying. By propping several bundles of grain together with the heads upright, the grain would dry more quickly for threshing. The mechanical reaper was a considerable improvement over the earlier method of cutting grain by hand with a sickle. Josh's grain had been drying for a while, and was now ready to have the grain threshed out of the enclosing hulls.

Josh walked over to Andrew to welcome him. "Beautiful day," he said. "Glad you could come."

Andrew nodded in agreement. "Sure is. It's good to get into the harness and do some work for a change."

Josh answered sympathetically, "I guess you've been through the mill the last couple of weeks. I'm glad your threshing was finished."

"Yes, it all worked out well," Andrew said. "But I'm glad it's behind us now." He pulled his team over to a row of stooks. Josh and his hired man started to throw sheaves on the wagon and Andrew piled them.

When they walked on to the next stook, Andrew gave his team the signal, "Giddy-up." They pulled ahead until he called, "Whoa."

"You've really got your team trained," Josh remarked. "That's nice. We don't need to get someone in to drive them."

"Jim McCraw trained them," Andrew replied modestly. "He did a decent job of it." He piled a few more stooks, then added with a chuckle, "They ran away from me once. A bee stung one of them in the haunch and he took off. Had quite a time getting them stopped."

Josh laughed. "It would take a lot to stop those two once they got going." He stopped for a moment and wiped the sweat off his forehead. "I saw a team run away with Jim one time. I was driving by when it happened." He laughed at the memory. "For some reason, he hadn't hitched them to a wagon and he was walking behind them, holding the reins. I never dared ask him what happened. The team just took off all of a sudden with Jim hanging on to the reins for dear life. Biggest steps I ever saw a man take, until he tripped and fell flat on his nose."

Andrew and the hired man joined in the laughter. "I suppose it was safer not to bring that up to Jim," Andrew said. "He's a friendly fellow, but it probably took him a while to get over that one. He trains his horses to a T, and he expects them to listen."

Their brief rest over, they returned to their work. By the time Andrew had stacked his wagon full of sheaves, the first team had returned with an empty wagon which took his place while Andrew went off to unload.

They finished the field at about 7:00 that evening. It was the last field of the year, and there was much backslapping in celebration. Josh's wife served a late supper before the neighbor men went home.

It had been a long day for Selina, and she was glad to see Andrew drive into the lane. She had just finished the chores, knowing he would be hot and tired when he got home. He was also dirty and covered with bits of grain and straw, but that didn't stop him from jumping off the wagon and giving Selina a big hug.

"I missed you today!" He grinned while she wrinkled her nose at him and dusted herself off.

"Well, it sure looks like it," she retorted. Then she added tact-fully, "Maybe you could dust yourself off with the broom before you come in."

He nodded. "I think I'll go for a dip in the creek. Might as well take my bath there instead of hauling water to the tub. Maybe you could get me some clean clothing while I put the horses in the barn."

Later, they sat in comfortable silence at the table. Andrew leaned back and relaxed. "Well, it's nice to have the last of the threshing done," he said. He walked over to the hand pump at the sink. "Want some more water?"

He pumped a few times until the water was cold, then refilled his tin mug. "Ah! That hits the spot," he said. "These modern conveniences are sure nice. I remember having to go out to the well for fresh water. Now we've got a pump right here in the kitchen." He drained his mug and smacked his lips. "Fresh water beats tea any time, after a hot day's work."

Selina smiled. "You're cheerful tonight, for a change," she remarked. "Welcome back. I've missed you."

Andrew sobered. "I know," he admitted. "It hasn't been an easy time. I think I just needed to find my way. The sun seemed brighter today than it has been for a long time. Even the grass was greener."

Selina nodded. "God does that for us," she said softly. "I'm so happy for you."

Several days later, Andrew finished his work early. "You know," he said thoughtfully, after supper, "I think I'm going to start reading that journal."

Selina looked up quickly. "That would be good. Your mother just asked me about it today."

"I'm not surprised," he replied. "I think she's pretty anxious to know what is in it. Poor woman, I think she suspects more than we realized. She has lived with these questions for years."

He got up, went to the bedroom, and returned with the journal, laying it on the table. "Do we have any writing paper?" he asked. "I might want to take some notes as I go, so I can keep track of any interesting entries."

Selina left him to his work, and returned to her dishes. She glanced at him occasionally, but left him to his thoughts. He took his time, making an occasional note or underlining an entry in the journal. His face was sober, but he didn't comment on what he was finding.

Finally, he closed the journal, tucking his notes inside it for a marker. "It's bedtime," he said.

Selina looked at his face, and swallowed any questions she had been ready to ask. Instead, she answered his comment. "I'm tired," she said. "It's been a long, tiring month."

Over the next few weeks, Andrew worked on the journal several evenings a week. It didn't seem to depress him as it had earlier, but still he didn't seem to want to talk about it. Selina didn't pressure him; she knew he would talk about it when he was ready.

Naomi asked her again several weeks later. "Has Andrew done anything with the journal yet?" Her voice was wistful. "Sometimes I feel like I just have to know what is in there. Other times I wish we had never found it." Her voice trailed off.

Selina nodded understandingly. "I'm sure the suspense must be getting to you," she said. "Andrew has been working on it. He is making notes as he goes. He hasn't said much about it, but I think he is almost to the end."

She took a deep breath. "He said he would like to get together with you and the girls and maybe ask Bishop George and his wife to come when we go through it. He said we might need George's advice."

"That's probably not a good sign," Naomi said soberly. "I'm not surprised, really. I just want to get it behind us so I can go on with life. I feel like I have a dark shadow hanging over me."

She sat back in her rocking chair. "I've been doing a lot of thinking lately about our marriage. I know I wasn't a perfect wife for Sylvester. I wish I could do some things over. But I must go on. I'm not that old yet, and I can't spend the rest of my days living in regret."

PART 2

Naomi's Perspective

"I was a typical girl when I was growing up. I had dreams of being a wife and mother. Unfortunately, reality wasn't quite what my dreams had led me to expect. Like usual, life had a way of bringing my dreams in line with reality. This part of the book is given from my point of view, during the years of my marriage to Sylvester.

I've been a widow now for almost as long as I was married. But I've never forgotten that first half of my adult life. Not a day goes by that I don't remember Sylvester. I still shed tears for him. But time has a way of healing even the deepest wounds, and I'm close to the end of my own life now. I don't want to waste the little time I have left by moping about the tough times I had as a wife and mother.

As Andrew already wrote in his introduction, I hope this book will help some other families out there. But I'm especially burdened for other women who might be facing the disappointment of life with an unfaithful husband. My heart goes out to you, if you are one of these. I want you to know that God can take you through even this, hard as it seems. Cling to God in your sorrows and accept whatever He allows to come into your life. God loves you and will see you through."

Naomi Martin

A Wedding Day

9

Now, may the God of Abraham, the God of Isaac, and the
God of Jacob bless this union, and what God has joined
together, let not man put asunder.
—*Marriage Vows, Mennonite Minister's Manual*

Sylvester's Journal
April 23, 1845:
Tomorrow is the big day! The next time I write in my
journal I'll be a married man. Feels strange in a way.
Am I giving up my freedom or gaining a relationship?
Maybe both, but I'm going to give it a good try. Naomi's
too nice a girl to let down.

Naomi was up early on the day of their wedding. But early as
she was, as she was dressing, she heard her mother bustling around
downstairs. "Oh, no, Mom and Dad are up already," she whispered.
"I need to get downstairs and help them." But she took a little time
to breathe a prayer before leaving her room.

God, please be with me today. And bless Sylvester too. Help me be a good wife for him. Her heart beat faster as she thought of what the day would mean. *By this afternoon I will no longer be Naomi Hershey; I'll be Mrs. Sylvester Martin.* But she didn't have time to ponder the thought. Already her mother was at the foot of the stairs.

"Naomi! It's time to get up! We don't have time to sleep in this morning, of all mornings." Naomi winced at the sharpness of her mother's voice. But that was just Mom; she often reacted that way to stress, and the marriage of her only daughter would really put her under pressure.

"I'm coming, Mom," she answered cheerily. "Don't work too hard, it's only a wedding." She grinned as she heard her mother's disgusted response.

By the time Naomi got down the steps, she heard kettles rattling furiously in the kitchen. At least no one could ever accuse her parents of being lazy. *Nor stingy,* she reminded herself. *They have gone all out for this wedding and are helping Sylvester and me get a good start in life.*

Naomi had barely reached the kitchen when her mother turned from the dishes she was washing. "When is Sylvester coming?" Her voice had moderated already. "We want to have breakfast ready by the time he gets here."

Naomi glanced at the clock. "He should be here in an hour or so," she replied. Her heart flip-flopped, but she didn't have time to mind her heart right then. "He said he'd be here by 7:00 or soon after." She picked up a tea towel to dry the dishes. "Simon and Adah will be here around the same time," she added.

Naomi was lost in thought when the sound of several buggies interrupted her reverie. She glanced at the clock. "They're early," she gasped, as her mother came bustling from the main bedroom.

"I figured they would be," her mother replied. "Neither Sylvester nor his father are known to be late." She looked Naomi over critically. "You had better put on a clean apron. You have messed that one up already. Go quickly before they come in."

Naomi scurried up the steps to her bedroom to get a clean apron.

She got back to the kitchen just as Sylvester's mother, Adah, stepped inside. "Well, it's a grand day for a wedding," she announced. "I hope you haven't gone to too much fuss about breakfast. Oatmeal mush is just fine."

Naomi grinned, but let her mother answer. "*Ach*, no. I just sliced up some leftover potatoes and fried them with some eggs and bacon. No fuss at all."

Sylvester and his father, Simon, came through the door just in time to hear this. "Now there's a woman with some good sense," Simon said, his booming voice carrying through the whole house. "Nothing like a solid breakfast to start the day off well."

Naomi nearly chuckled at the triumphant look on her mother's face, then turned to finish setting the table. *Simon knows how to make a woman feel good*, she thought. *That'll make Mom's day. She likes to be recognized for her cooking abilities.*

Breakfast was a resounding success, but then the real work started. They needed to move the furniture to make room for the backless benches the church used for weddings and funerals. Naomi's brothers and their wives showed up soon after breakfast, and the women got busy with preparations for the meal that would be served after the wedding. The men moved furniture and carried in benches.

"It was easier in the old days," Naomi's father commented. "When we got married, we just went to the bishop's house, said our vows, and came back home for a family dinner." He shook his head. "Things have really changed. Next thing you know, we'll be having weddings in the church house like the heathen do." He quickly changed his tone when he saw his wife's sharp glance. "Well, I meant the Methodists," he corrected himself sheepishly. Naomi's oldest brother Adam had joined the Methodists a while back, and her mother was still sensitive about it.

But Sylvester's father picked up the conversation. "Heathen they are." His voice boomed, penetrating the noise around them. "It's about time we got that clear to our young folks. Camp meetings and immersions, being baptized by the Spirit, and all the rest of that nonsense. They can do as they like, but it is time for them to stop reaching into our church for people. What was good enough for our parents should be good enough for us."

Naomi's back stiffened. It was scarcely over a year since her brother Reuben had died from falling out of the haymow while in a drunken stupor. The reality of his death had stopped the whole family in its tracks, and it was after Reuben's death that Adam was "saved" at a Methodist revival. *I think he's happier than any of the rest of us,* she thought. *We Mennonites aren't doing such a wonderful job of helping our people find God. I'm sure Reuben wasn't ready to die, and I wouldn't have been either, at that point.*

Both Naomi and Sylvester had asked for baptism some months after Reuben's accident. That was one reason they could have a regular house wedding. Many couples went to local Protestant ministers to get married. Mennonite leaders refused to marry couples who weren't members.

I'm glad Sylvester's father[1] *is marrying us instead of the bishop.* Naomi shivered. *The bishop is so stern, and he notices every little thing. He would surely find something wrong with my dress.* Simon could be the same way, but he had never picked on her. In fact, she felt that he got a bit too familiar with her at times.

The morning passed quickly and people were starting to arrive for the wedding. Since the event was held in the home, it wasn't a large wedding. Seventy or eighty guests were invited, mostly close friends and relatives. Naomi and several of her friends had dressed for the wedding in her little bedroom, and they watched through the window as people arrived.

They had invited some younger boys as hostlers. It was their job to put the horses into the barn and feed them, as well as do any other necessary chores. After the wedding, they would hitch up the horses and bring the buggies around for the owners when they left.

---

[1] In the Mennonite Church at this time, bishops and ministers performed marriage ceremonies.

Of course, the hostlers expected a tip for their services. Anyone who refused to pay might find their buggy hidden in the orchard, or even minus a wheel. Some good-natured banter took place about prices, but people considered it part of the day's fun.

The wedding party gathered in Naomi's bedroom while the rest of the guests were being seated downstairs. Naomi noticed that Sylvester was quieter than normal. *I often don't know what he's thinking. I hope he will learn to share his heart with me after we're married.* The thought of marriage still scared her. She shivered again.

Her best friend Katie saw and smiled. "Are you cold?" Her voice was mischievous. "Or just scared?" Katie grinned at her, and Elsie, who had married a few months earlier, gave her a wink from across the room. Naomi didn't get a chance to reply. A sharp rap at the door brought them all to attention.

"Time for you to come down." The usher was all business. "Everyone is seated and ready to start. Follow me, two by two."

Now Naomi's heart really started to flutter, and she wondered again what Sylvester was thinking. But he didn't look at her. They were the second couple in line, and the rest followed them. She took a deep breath as they entered the main room. The front rows had been left empty for the wedding party.

A long sermon, delivered in German, preceded the marriage ceremony. Sylvester's father was at his best (or worst, depending on your perspective) and his booming voice grated on Naomi's nerves. *I'm sure everyone could hear him at half the volume,* she thought. She tried to concentrate on what he was saying, but he was in the middle of a story from his own childhood. *How is that supposed to help Sylvester and me get started with our home?* she wondered. Overall, she was grateful when he finished, and they all knelt in silent prayer.

Then the fateful moment arrived. Sylvester's father reached into the breast pocket of his suit and, with a flourish, pulled out a well-worn copy of a German minister's manual. He flipped through the pages until he found the section for the marriage ceremony. Many ministers and bishops could have performed the whole ceremony by memory, but it was the accepted practice to read it.

"It was announced three times publicly in the congregation that Sylvester Martin and Naomi Hershey desire to marry. Up to the present no objection has been made . . ."

His words seemed to come from a long distance away, but Naomi managed to stand at the right time and give the proper responses to his questions, though later she could not remember what she said and when.

Then came the moment everyone was waiting for. "You may join your right hands," Sylvester's father proclaimed. Naomi noticed that Sylvester's hand felt clammy and shook a little. *He's as scared as I am.* For some reason, the thought surprised her.

The minister placed his hand on their clasped hands and continued to read. "The God of Abraham, the God of Isaac, and the God of Jacob be with you . . ." Naomi fought a moment of panic and pushed aside the impulse to run while she still could. Then, "Go forth as husband and wife: fear God and keep His commandments."

She heard Sylvester sigh with relief. *He's glad it's almost over. And so am I.*

Naomi and Sylvester watched the last of their friends leave from her parents' front porch. Supper had occupied part of the evening. That was followed by singing, and then the older people went home while the young folks played games. Naomi's parents had gone to bed hours ago, and the hostlers had finished their work and left after dividing their gains. Sylvester had liberally topped off their earnings. Deserved or not, that one action gave him a reputation for generosity among some people for years to come.

It was a beautiful evening, with a full moon lighting up the sky. They were alone for the first time since they were married, and they weren't quite sure how to act. Neither of them knew how it happened, but suddenly Naomi noticed they were holding hands. Even in the moonlight, Sylvester's deep blue eyes seemed to look beyond her. What was he thinking? She could not read his mind like her mother read her father's mind. Surely by the time they were married a few months or years that would change.

Naomi Learns Some of the Facts of Life

10

A dream you dream alone is only a dream.

Naomi and Sylvester were married on a Tuesday. Sylvester went back to his farm on Wednesday morning, while Naomi stayed behind to help clean up. On Thursday Sylvester returned for Naomi and her belongings. Both sets of parents joined them at their new home, to help set up the furniture Naomi's parents had given her. Finally, by Thursday evening, Naomi and Sylvester were alone in the house where they would spend their married life together.

Sylvester and Naomi stood on the front porch and watched everyone leave. Naomi waved until everyone was out of sight. Sylvester leaned against the porch railing with his thumbs hooked into the waistband of his trousers. "Well, I guess that's that," he said, seating himself on the porch steps. He patted the spot beside him, an unspoken invitation for her to join him. Naomi settled beside him, feeling shy and awkward. She and Sylvester had kept company for several years, but tonight she felt as if she hardly knew him.

They watched the sun sinking in the west. The sunset spilled a panorama of golden fire across the horizon, and Naomi caught her breath. "It's beautiful," she whispered. "I hope our marriage can be like that."

Sylvester looked at her curiously, then back at the sunset. Sure enough, he noticed, it was pretty. He had sat at this spot dozens of evenings, enjoying the cool evening breezes before he went to bed. He hadn't particularly thought of the sunset before, but with Naomi sitting at his side, it did stir a sympathetic warmth in his heart. But his taciturn personality wouldn't let him voice it.

"Well, I guess our marriage will be what we make of it," he remarked matter-of-factly, as if he had been discussing the price of lumber for his furniture shop.

Naomi drew back a little and her face clouded. "Yes, I suppose so," she answered. But her heart cried, *Why can't we share the beauty together? Doesn't he care any more than that?*

Sylvester noticed her involuntary reaction and realized too late how his reply had sounded. He drew back too, then got to his feet.

"Well, we might as well go to bed," he said tonelessly. "I've got a fair bit to do in the morning."

Funny thing happened last night. Naomi said some-thing about our marriage turning out as beautiful as the sunset. Strange idea. I hadn't even noticed the sunset, but she was right, it was pretty. I didn't know what to say. Guess I botched it. She was rather quiet, for our first night in our home together. I'll have to pay more atten-tion to her feelings.

According to his journal, Sylvester felt bad about the exchange, but that didn't keep him from sleeping. He was soon snoring, while Naomi lay stiffly beside him. The moon rose and finally set again before she dropped into a restless sleep. She wasn't used to sharing a bed, and she was afraid that she would wake Sylvester if she tossed and turned. But his lack of sympathy with her admiration of the sunset had hurt more than she would admit even to herself.

Naomi was very tired in the morning, but if Sylvester noticed, he didn't comment. In fact, he didn't say much of anything. But he did turn to her before going out the door to do his morning chores.

"I guess you know where most of the things are for making breakfast. The oatmeal is in the pantry, and there's honey in the dumbwaiter."

Naomi pulled her wits together enough to remember that there were several ways to make porridge. "How do you like your oatmeal?" she asked as he reached for the door. "Shall I make it with milk or with water? And do you want coffee? Or tea?"

Sylvester hesitated. "Well, water's cheaper," he said. "But we've got our own milk, and oatmeal is better that way. I think there is still some dried garden tea in the pantry. My mother planted some in her garden and keeps bringing it over."

Well, I guess I'll use milk if he likes it better that way, Naomi thought as she watched him stride toward the barn. In the growing daylight, she felt better and was eager to get their relationship started in a good direction. *Maybe he didn't know what to say last night. I know he doesn't notice things like sunsets and flowers.*

Sylvester, too, was more cheerful when he returned from the barn. He even helped her set the table. He dished out a bowl of porridge to cool, then liberally coated it with honey. "Always did like my mush sweet," he said between mouthfuls. Then, he added as an afterthought, "But I was thinking about the milk. I can sell lots of milk in town, so maybe we should mostly use water for the porridge." But he seemed to remember her response of last evening, and added, "It's sure good this way, though. Maybe we could do it this way on Sundays."

Naomi poured a cup of tea for each of them, then sat across the table from him again. "I've got a lot to learn about what you like and don't like," she said hesitantly. "What do you want for lunch and supper? What are you used to having?"

Sylvester looked startled. "Well, I went home for supper once or twice a week and my mother would send along some leftovers. I've never really put a lot of thought into eating. I'll leave that up to you, I guess. If you need groceries, I can pick them up when I go to town." He hesitated and seemed to be choosing his words carefully. "I'm making payments on the place, so I'd like to live as cheaply as we can.

"Well, I've got a cupboard I need to finish today for a customer, so I guess I'll get to work." He got to his feet and pulled his hat off the hook beside the door. "If you have more questions about things, you can come out to the shop. Then he added awkwardly, "I'd be happy to show you around. You've never been in my shop."

Naomi had much to think about that morning as she went through the pantry and the dumbwaiter to see what she could put together for an attractive noon meal. *Hmm, I never realized Sylvester was so money-conscious. I'll have to be careful not to cost him too much.* She shook her head ruefully. *I hope he doesn't consider me a liability.*

She found her way to the basement where she discovered canned applesauce, fresh apples, and potatoes. Pleased with her find, she decided to make potato soup for lunch. *There's some cream in the dumbwaiter,* she remembered. *I'll cube the potatoes and boil them, then add some cream and butter. And we can have applesauce for dessert. I'll have to make some pies so we have something special to serve if someone drops in to visit.*

Glad for a chance to be useful, she stoked the fire in the cook-stove and put water on to boil while she peeled and cut the potatoes. Sylvester came in for lunch promptly at noon and she greeted him cheerfully.

He sniffed the air appreciatively. "Well, you seem to have found some things to make for lunch," he said. "Makes me hungry just to smell it." It was the closest thing to praise he had given her yet. He paused between bites. "My pa stopped by this morning and invited us over for supper this evening. I told him we would be there about 6:30. That way you won't need to make supper tonight."

He pulled his hat off the hook and headed out the door. "That was a good lunch," he said over his shoulder. Then he added, "You could sweep up some of the sawdust in the shop this afternoon, if you were looking for something to do."

Naomi had planned to do some cleaning that afternoon. It was customary to clean the house at the end of the week in case visitors stopped by on Sunday. *But it seems he wants to show me his shop,* she thought. *It's only Friday, and I can get the cleaning done tomorrow.*

She pulled on her bonnet. It was a beautiful day, but she noticed some weeds in the flowerbeds her mother-in-law had planted earlier that spring. *I should look after those flowerbeds,* she thought. She bent to pull a weed. *But I guess that can wait until next week.* She paused before crossing the lane to Sylvester's shop. It was a good feeling to have her own house and yard to look after. And for once, she wouldn't have her mother hanging over her to make sure her work was good enough. Hopefully, Sylvester's parents wouldn't consider her too lazy to look after her duties.

She opened the shop door to the sound of a table saw. She had expected the shop to be dark, but it wasn't. Sylvester had installed extra windows, especially in the areas where he did most of his work. The shop appeared tidy, even to her inexperienced eyes. It was easy to see that Sylvester took pride in his shop.

The table saw stopped its shrieking and Sylvester turned to greet her. "Broom's in the closet." He gestured to a tall cupboard beside the door. "You can start back here. I've got to paint this cabinet today yet, and that way the dust will have a chance to settle before I start."

This wasn't quite the greeting that Naomi had expected. *So all he wanted was some help cleaning up his shop, when I could be cleaning the house,* she thought, a little miffed. She had expected him to give her a guided tour and show her his equipment. But he was already picking up another piece of lumber and the table saw let out another high-pitched wail as he started to cut again. She swallowed her feelings and took an old broom from the closet.

Naomi had eaten at Sylvester's home during their courtship, but going there as his wife was different. She felt a little jittery as he dropped her off at the door of the old house.

Sylvester's mother was waiting for her at the door. "Well, come right in and make yourself at home! You can put your coat and bonnet on our bed."

Adah was a good cook, and she was at her best that night. Supper was a grand spread, with potatoes, peas, canned sausage, and bread still warm from the oven. This was an unusually lavish meal for a weekday. Even for a Sunday, it would have been on the extravagant side, especially since she topped it off with stewed apple *schnitz* followed by shoofly pie. Adah kept pushing seconds on them until Naomi was so full she almost groaned. Sylvester seemed to enjoy the meal even though he had told Naomi earlier he didn't pay much attention to food.

"Take some more," Adah urged him for the third time. "I know Naomi hasn't had a chance to do any baking. And she didn't have a chance to do a lot of canning, either. You didn't give her much notice for getting married."

Sylvester rolled his eyes at his mother's constant chatter. "Naomi wanted to get married as much as I did," he replied. "We'll survive until she can do her canning this summer."

He glanced at Naomi out of the corner of his eye, before adding, "If we run out we can always come here for supper. A meal like this should keep us going for a day or two."

"Well, I'll pack up some of the leftovers," his mother said. "Don't want you two starving over there."

This was going a little overboard in Naomi's opinion, but she didn't dare speak up. *My parents gave us lots of canned food,* she thought. *It might not be as fancy as this, but it will surely keep us from starving.*

Apparently Sylvester also thought his mother had gone far enough. "Naomi's parents gave us lots of canned fruit and vegetables and some canned meat. We are far from starving. And Naomi is a good cook. The potato soup we had for lunch was good."

His father seemed to think it was time to change the subject. "Let's return thanks," he said, and everyone bowed their heads in silent prayer.[1]

Several weeks later, Naomi was cleaning the parlor when Sylvester came into the house for a paper he had forgotten. He unlocked his rolltop desk then noticed that Naomi was watching him curiously.

"Why do you keep your desk locked?" she asked. "I could clean it for you if you would leave it unlocked."

Sylvester looked up, and she sensed that she had said the wrong thing. "I prefer to clean my desk myself," he informed her stiffly.

She got the distinct feeling that he really meant, *I don't need anyone snooping through my papers.*

His answer stunned Naomi and he seemed to feel the need to explain. "I don't like having my papers shuffled around by anyone else. I put them where they are for a reason, and I don't want anyone moving them." His voice softened when he saw the look on her face. "My father always kept his desk locked."

He turned his back and locked the desk. Naomi watched him walk out the door. *Maybe your father was like that, but my father shared everything with my mother. I assumed we would do the same. But Sylvester seems to feel I was trying to snoop.* She dropped her cleaning rag and walked

---

[1] Ministers were expected to say grace before and after meals, especially when they were visiting or had company.

to the window where she stared unseeing at the beautiful orchard. *I wonder what he has in his desk that he doesn't want me to see. And why?*

She went to the kitchen to start supper. Normally she enjoyed preparing meals for Sylvester. Despite his avowed indifference to food, he seemed to enjoy her cooking. But tonight the joy was gone.

It was a quiet meal. Naomi tried to eat, but soon gave up. If Sylvester noticed that something was amiss, he didn't let on. But he didn't talk either. As Naomi watched him, it dawned on her that she was seeing a pattern. *Every time he gets upset at me or realizes he has hurt me, he goes quiet like this. I wonder why he is paranoid about showing his feelings or admitting that he was wrong. But at least he realizes that he hurt me, and he feels bad about it. Or I guess he does.*

After supper, Sylvester unfolded a newspaper he had bought in town and spread it on the table. Naomi watched him, wondering how long he would go until he said something. Usually he at least remarked about some news item or other, but not tonight.

I wonder if he's even reading, she thought. *He's been looking at that paper for over ten minutes and hasn't flipped a page.* By now she was sure that he felt badly about how he had treated her, but didn't know what to do about it. *I wonder if this is how his father handled disagreements with his mother.*

She shook off the question and mentally squared her shoulders. *Well, I guess I'll have to make the first move.* She cleared her throat timidly, hoping she wasn't doing the wrong thing.

"Sylvester . . ." She paused as his head jerked up. Evidently, he hadn't expected her to say anything. "I'm sorry for upsetting you," she continued softly. "I really do want to be a good wife for you, rather than a nuisance. I won't snoop into your things if you don't want me to. But you don't need to lock me out of your desk. All you have to do is tell me and I'll leave it alone."

Sylvester had a hard time meeting her eyes. Perhaps apologies were outside his frame of reference.

I really can't see either of his parents apologizing to the other, she thought involuntarily. *They probably just give each other the silent treatment until they get over their huff. Well, I don't intend to act that way.*

He dropped his eyes to his paper again. "I suppose I was curious what you do at your desk so often. But I'll honor your wishes. I just wish you would trust me." She muffled a sob as she finished.

Sylvester fumbled a little with his newspaper. "Well, um . . . I guess that's okay then." He changed the subject. "It's early yet. How about we hitch up and drive over to your parents for a while?" It was an attempt at reconciliation, and she accepted it graciously.

"I would like that," she said gently. "We haven't been back very often since we were married."

Naomi was reminiscing a bit tonight. She looked a bit wistful. I can tell she wishes we were closer. She told me about some of her teenage struggles. Then she talked about her brother Reuben's death and the turmoil it put her in. She said it was a good thing because it got her thinking about death and God and all that. She talked to her grandmother about it, and they looked at the Bible together. She seems to be at peace about God, and she isn't scared at the idea of dying any more. Almost asked her about it, but decided not to. Maybe she'll talk more about it on her own. Wish I could find an answer that easy. I never like to think about dying. Gives me a creepy feeling, somehow.

Andrew

11

For this child I prayed; and the LORD hath given me my petition which I asked of him (1 Samuel 1:27).

I always wanted to have a family. I love children. I thought it might help Sylvester be more open with me if we had a baby. But it didn't work out that way. The Woodpile Incident, as it came to be known in my mind, happened a few months before our first child was born. —Naomi Martin

Naomi stood and stared at the pile of wood outside their woodshed. Sylvester had recently bought several wagonloads of wood from a neighbor and dumped it in their front yard. This innocent action was rapidly turning into the biggest test of their marriage so far. *Surely, Sylvester doesn't expect me to pile all that wood into the woodshed by myself,* she thought. *That will take me weeks to finish. And I'm not feeling too well these days. After all, I am expecting a child. He couldn't have been serious.*

But Naomi found out at lunchtime that Sylvester had been serious. He wasn't very happy when he noticed she hadn't been working on the wood pile. "It would be nice if you could get at that wood pile," he said stiffly. "It would be easier today since the weather is warmer. If you spend an hour or two a day working at it, you could clean it up in a couple of weeks."

She hesitated before replying. She knew that Sylvester didn't like "yes, but" answers. But surely . . .

"Sylvester, what about the baby?" she said. "Couldn't that harm it?"

"My father used to say a baby would be stronger if the mother kept active. I'm thinking it would be good for you." He got up from the table and turned abruptly toward the door. "I would like it piled inside before we get more rain." He took his hat from its peg beside the door and was gone before she could reply.

The job was just as hard as it looked. By the time Naomi had carried five or six armloads inside, the sweat was dripping from her forehead, in spite of the cool fall weather. *That pile looks just as big as it did when I started,* she told herself. Her heart sank. *This will take a long, long time.*

She filled her arms with wood again, and started her seventh trip to the woodshed. She didn't hear the footsteps until a voice spoke behind her. "Naomi Martin! What do you think you're doing?" She dropped her load and turned to face her brother Isaac and his wife.

"I'm moving this woodpile into the woodshed," she answered evenly. "What did you think I was doing?"

"You had better not let Sylvester catch you at that," Isaac said. "He would have a fit to see you working like that."

"He would have a fit if I didn't." The bitter words were out before she could stop them. "He thinks more work would be good for me."

The silence that followed was deafening. Her sister-in-law gasped. But her brother almost blew up. "Where is he? In his shop? I'm going to have a word with him about this."

Naomi paled. "Oh, please don't," she begged. "He'll think I tattled."

Isaac stopped. "That's true," he agreed. "But I'll do something. You'll harm yourself and more if you do this."

Naomi discovered the following afternoon what her brother meant by "doing something." She had finished her lunch dishes and was tying her kerchief when she heard horses' hooves. Puzzled, she opened the door to see who was coming, and saw several buggies pulling up to the hitching posts by Sylvester's shop. Her brothers Adam and Isaac and their hired men jumped out of the buggies. They tied their horses and headed toward the woodpile.

Several of the men saw her standing on the porch and waved. "Hi, Sis," Isaac called cheerfully. "Show us where this wood is supposed to go. We'll have that pile moved in a jiffy."

And they did. Sylvester discreetly stayed out of sight in his shop, though Naomi was sure she saw him looking out the window several times. Her brothers let her help, but monitored her efforts closely.

"No way," one of them informed her when she bent over to pick up a sizeable chunk. "That piece is too big for you. Stick to the smaller pieces if you want to help."

She did want to help. For one thing, she didn't get to see her brothers very often, so this was a treat for her. And for another, she wanted to be sure she could tell Sylvester she had helped. *I wonder how he's going to react to this,* she thought as she picked up several smaller chunks of wood. *I hope he doesn't think I asked them to come. Surely he knows me better than that.*

Sylvester did have the grace to come out of his shop when they had finished. Naomi saw him thanking the men for their work. She also saw her oldest brother Adam pull Sylvester aside and give him some pointed advice. At least she presumed that was what he did— no one ever told her. Sylvester didn't mention the wood pile again, nor did she. But never again did he ask her to pile wood.

Naomi's brothers and their hired hands stopped by and piled the wood into the woodshed. She helped them, and

I doubt she had asked for their help. But it did sort of make me look like an idiot. I think her brothers were a bit steamed up at the idea that I asked her to do that, but they were careful what they said. Adam, her oldest brother, told me a few things before he left, though. He was nice about it, but told me that no woman expecting a baby should be required to work like that. Said it could harm the baby and the mother both. He told me that if I didn't have time to do my work, to let him know and he'll send someone over to help me for a few days. Maybe it was a bit extreme. I don't want word going around that I'm making a slave out of my wife.

Andrew was born about three months after the woodpile incident. Naomi was sure being a father would change Sylvester. And he did seem to change a little, at least for a while. He even hired a girl to help Naomi for about six weeks, though that might have been because of his mother's prodding.

But Naomi soon discovered that Sylvester didn't like to have his sleep interrupted by a crying baby. Especially after the novelty of being a father had worn off.

Waah! Naomi awoke with a start. *I must quiet Andrew before he wakes Sylvester.*

Sleepily, she lifted Andrew from the cradle and stumbled out into the chilly kitchen. With one hand, she stirred up some glowing embers in the cookstove and added several pieces of wood. She pulled the wooden rocker close to the stove and tried to comfort her wailing baby. *He's probably got a wet diaper, but I'll try to warm him up a bit before I change him.* She cuddled him close, wrapping the woolen blanket that served as a chair cover closely around herself and the baby.

She awoke with a jerk from a sound sleep when the bedroom door opened. Sylvester emerged, still rubbing his eyes. "I'm going out to do chores," he announced. "Could you have breakfast ready when I come back in? I've got a lot of work to do today." He brushed past her and out the door before she could reply.

Naomi gritted her teeth, then let her shoulders sag in resignation. *I have been late with breakfast every morning this week, but what am I supposed to do if I need to feed Andrew first thing in the morning? My father used to make breakfast for himself sometimes so my mother could rest.* She knew, however, that she might as well expect the sun to come up in the west before that happened. She quietly laid the still sleeping baby in his cradle and stirred up the fire again. *I wish I could make eggs and fried potatoes for breakfast,* she thought wistfully. *But we sell all our eggs, so it'll have to be mush again. At least Sylvester likes mush.*

Breakfast was almost ready when Sylvester returned from the barn. He nodded in satisfaction as she brought the steaming pot to the table. But a howl from the bedroom drowned out his comment and Naomi jumped up to get the baby. By the time she returned to the table, Sylvester had finished his breakfast, and her mush was cold.

"What ails him anyway?" Sylvester asked. "He's been a real grouch for the past week."

"I think he's teething," Naomi defended. "His gums seem to be hurting, and he's about the right age for that."

"Well, I wish he'd get on with it," Sylvester muttered. "He sure seems to be taking his time."

Naomi's back stiffened and she replied evenly, "I'm sure you did the same thing when you were six months old. This is simply the way life is with a baby in the house."

Sylvester noticed her reaction and refrained from replying. But he slammed the door harder than usual as he left the kitchen on his way to the shop.

Andrew's first tooth popped through a day later, and even Sylvester took time to look at it. He seemed pleased, though he didn't say much. His mother made up for it when his parents stopped in for a few minutes later that day.

"He has his first tooth," Adah crowed, as if she were personally responsible for it. "Sylvester, you have to write this in your journal."

Naomi's brow furrowed. *Journal? I must have misunderstood her. Sylvester surely isn't the type to keep a journal.* She passed it off and forgot it in the excitement of the moment.

Eventually, teething time passed, as it always does. Even Sylvester noticed that Andrew was happier again. He stopped by his son's crib one day and picked him up, while Naomi finished setting the table for lunch.

"Well, young fellow, how are you? No teeth bugging you today?" Andrew smiled and gurgled in reply. Sylvester bounced him on his knee a few times and smiled at the baby's reaction. "Well, well," he said cheerfully. "You're getting to be a big boy, aren't you?"

Naomi watched the exchange out of the corner of her eye while she carried the potato soup to the table. *It's nice to see Sylvester paying some attention to Andrew. I really wonder what he'd be like if he allowed himself to relax and enjoy life. He used to be more like this when we were courting, especially at first. I wonder what changed him? It's as if some kind of guilt or bad memories are bothering him. I wish he'd tell me about it.*

It was a cheerful, relaxing meal for a change. Sylvester finished his potato soup and apple sauce, then sat back in his chair, cleaning his teeth with a toothpick.

"Just finished up that big order of cabinets and counters for the new hardware store in town," he said. "I'm going to deliver them this afternoon and take the money to the bank. Give me a list of what you want me to pick up at the store."

He sat back in his chair and stretched his arms. "Always a good feeling to get to the end of a big project." Leaning over the crib, he tweaked Andrew under the chin. "You look after your mama while I'm gone." Andrew grinned and gurgled.

Sylvester pulled on his parka and turned to go out the door. "I'm all loaded. Just need to hitch the horses, so if you can get me that list, I'll head out in about twenty minutes." Over his shoulder, he added, almost as an afterthought, "I might be a bit late getting home, so you might want to start supper later."

Naomi watched him go. *I wish he'd always be like this,* she thought. *We could be very happy together. I wonder if he'll still be cheerful when he comes home.* She pondered that while she found a pencil and a piece of paper for her list. *I wonder if going to town is part of his problem. He often comes home upset.* It was a new thought, and she kept toying with it through the afternoon.

True to his word, Sylvester was about an hour late getting home. Naomi had just enough time to set the table for supper while he unhitched his team from the wagon he used to deliver his cabinets.

He carried in the groceries, kicking the snow off his boots as he came through the door. "Snowing again," he remarked. "Might be in for a long winter. Hardly ever have this much snow in November."

Sylvester didn't have much to say during supper. He didn't even notice when Andrew fell asleep in his play pen. Naomi noticed all this, and thought again of her questions.

"Did something go wrong in town?" she asked. "You seem really quiet tonight."

Sylvester looked startled. "No. Just tired, I guess."

"You seem . . ." she hesitated a little. "You seem so blue, as if you had something on your mind." She would have said more, but his face hardened as if he was resisting her sympathy, so she got to her feet instead.

"I'll clear the table and do the dishes. We can get to bed earlier tonight. Andrew seems to be off to sleep for the night."

Sylvester cleared his throat as if he were going to reply, then changed his mind and got to his feet. "Going to do some bookkeeping," he mumbled over his shoulder as he opened the door to the parlor.

Naomi watched him go, noting the slump in his shoulders. *Something happened in town,* she told herself. *He is tired but it is more than that. I wish he would talk about it. I'm sure I could help him with his trouble, whatever it is.*

She continued to turn it over in her mind while she cleared the table and washed the dishes. Outside, the weather turned nasty, and sleet rattled against the windows. She shuddered a little as she imagined how it would feel to get caught outside. *I'm glad Sylvester got home before this started.*

Andrew slept soundly the whole night. But Sylvester was restless and kept tossing and turning enough to keep Naomi from sleeping soundly. He must have been dreaming, because he kept muttering in his sleep. She wasn't sure, but she thought she heard him swear once. Another time he whispered something that sounded like, "Wish I could forget."

It all added to the puzzle. *What took place in town?* she wondered. *He usually sleeps like a log once he gets to bed. But he's in a real turmoil tonight.*

Sylvester seemed more like himself in the morning. In fact, he put forth real effort to be cheerful, though Naomi was pretty sure it was mostly pretense. "Had a lousy night," he said, running his hand through his hair. He looked out the window. The weather hadn't changed much from the night before and he shook his head as another gust of wind blew sleet against the glass.

"Glad I don't have to go to town today," he said. "I'd better get a fire started in the shop when I go out to do chores. It'll be cold out there this morning."

Makes me feel guilty to come home to my family and pretend nothing is wrong. Naomi was really watching me tonight, almost as if she was trying to read my mind. Glad she can't.

The next month was up and down. Sometimes Sylvester seemed to relax and was cheerful. More often, he was moody and glum. He made several trips to town and Naomi smelled liquor on his breath once. But she never could tell for sure if there was a pattern that connected his moodiness with his trips to town. Several times she saw a correlation, but other times she didn't. As time went on, Sylvester sensed she was watching him, and he tightened up even more.

I need to stop watching him. Sylvester was becoming more distant. *I'll just have to give it over to God and pray for him more rather than pestering him about his trips to town.*

True to her vow, she did her best to ignore Sylvester's trips to town. Unless he brought up the subject, she left it alone. But she prayed a lot for him, especially while he was in town.

A few months later, Sylvester told her at lunchtime that he was going to town later that day. "I'll leave about 3:30 or so," he added. "I want to get a new file to sharpen my table saw and stop in at one of the new building sites in town to see if they need any cupboards or counters. I'm almost caught up with my orders."

Naomi noticed that he seemed to be watching for her reaction. But all she said was, "Could you stop in at the general store and get me some black thread? I need to catch up on my mending pile and I'm out of thread." He pursed his lips but nodded.

I wonder if his troubles have something to do with that store? I'll need to do some strong praying this afternoon. Either her intuition was wrong, or her prayers helped, because Sylvester was cheerful when he returned from town.

"Well, I got a couple of new jobs this afternoon," he announced as he came in for a late supper. "I stopped at two new building sites, and both owners ordered cupboards and some wardrobes."

Naomi smiled at his news. "That's great. How soon do they need them?"

"As soon as possible," said Sylvester, spreading butter on a slice of fresh, warm, homemade bread. "I like fresh bread," he commented. "Especially straight out of the oven on a chilly day."

Naomi nodded, then asked, "Did you get my thread?"

He nodded. "I almost forgot. Got to the store just as the owner was locking up. All his workers had left, so he just grabbed a spool off the rack and told me to pay for it the next time around."

Sylvester dug into his coat pocket and pulled out a spool of thread before he went outside again. "Just got to finish up the chores," he said. "Won't take long, maybe three-quarters of an hour or so."

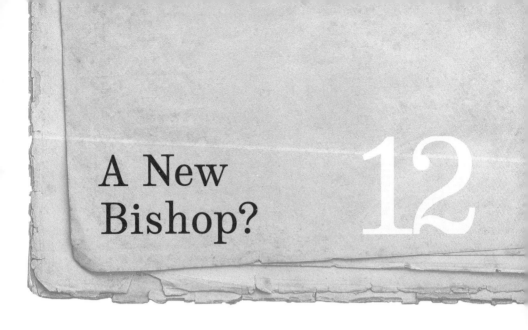

A New Bishop?

For a bishop must be blameless, as the steward of God;
not self-willed, not soon angry (Titus 1:7).

On Monday morning, about six months later, Sylvester had just finished the last of his mush. He leaned back in his chair and stretched. "Sundays are bad for a person," he remarked. "You never feel like working on a Monday morning."

Naomi raised her eyebrows a little. "You could take the day off and help me in the garden," she suggested, a glint of humor in her eyes.

The front legs of Sylvester's chair came down with a thump. "Nope," he declared. "I'm not that far gone yet." But he smiled despite himself.

Naomi had just opened her mouth to reply when they both heard it. A horse and buggy was coming in the lane, and coming rapidly. Sylvester jumped up. "Someone's on the road early," he said. "I hope nothing is wrong."

He pulled open the door and stepped out on the front porch.

Naomi was right behind him. The horse was foaming under its harness, a sure sign that the driver had been pushing it hard.

The driver was Jonathan, a young man who lived on the far side of the district. "Can you get my horse a drink of water?" he asked. "Give it to him slow. He's pretty hot."

"Sure," Sylvester said. "Bring him right over here to the watering trough. The water has been sitting all night and it's not cold. That will be better for him than cold water from the well.

"What's happening? I take it you're not just out on a morning joy ride?" Naomi was glad that Sylvester asked, because she was burning with curiosity.

"Bishop Amos died during the night," Jonathan replied. "I'm out helping to spread the word."

Naomi gasped. "Amos was in church yesterday morning," she said. "He seemed okay then."

"They figure it was a heart attack," Jonathan replied. "He had been having a lot of chest pains in the past months and any little exertion made him puff. The other ministers were trying to persuade him to ordain another bishop so he could slow down."

Sylvester huffed. "He didn't want to take any chances on the wrong person taking his place. He kept his thumb down pretty tight on the church." His voice was tinged with sarcasm.

Jonathan seemed to agree. "Well, we don't have any choice but to have an ordination now," he remarked. "Actually, it might be okay to have some new blood, someone with a few different ideas."

Sylvester shrugged. "Not a big chance of that," he noted. "George is about the only one who would dare to do anything much different. Most of the rest are like my father—they just want to stick to the old ways, no matter what. Can't have the Methodists rubbing off on us, you know."

Jonathan eyed him, as if wondering what he could safely say. "Well, the old ways haven't worked very well for some of us. We've lost a dozen families to the Methodists in the last few years, and others will be going too. It might be better to change a few things so we can keep our people together."

Sylvester raised his eyebrows. "You sound like John Oberholzer," he said. "I hear he's trying to get the ministers' conference to start taking written minutes and have a written constitution. That seems pretty high-minded. It might not be like the Methodists so much. But it is following the road of the Papists."[1]

Jonathan seemed suddenly anxious to get going. "Well, Oberholzer isn't likely to get far with his ideas.[2] Nor will our church change much if he does get them through. I would take Methodists before the Papists any day, myself."

He jumped back into his buggy. "Got to keep going. The funeral is on Wednesday and viewing is this evening and all day tomorrow at his home. See you then." Jonathan swung the buggy around and headed out the lane, his horse tugging at the reins and anxious to run.

Sylvester watched him leave. "My father would have a fit if he heard someone talking like that," he noted. "Jonathan is a good fellow, though. He will be a preacher himself someday at the rate he's going. That is, if he doesn't leave for the Methodists first."

"My brother Adam joined the Methodists," Naomi commented mildly from the porch, where she had been listening silently. "He is a lot happier there than he ever was with our church."

"Well, Adam was always pretty 'holier-than-thou.' He wouldn't take a drink or smoke a cigar or take a chew of tobacco, not even to save his life." Sylvester walked across the lane toward his shop. "Got to get busy. We'll have to go all the way over to the viewing tomorrow and then to the funeral on Wednesday. That will really cut into my working time this week."

Naomi watched him go, waiting to go back into the house until he had entered his shop. It was time to get Andrew up and give him

---

[1] An old term referring to the Catholic Church.

[2] This was a true prophecy. The Mennonite leadership rejected Oberholzer's ideas about a year later, and he led a group of around six congregations out of the main conference. He started his own group, known for years as the General Mennonite Conference.

his breakfast. But the discussion lingered in her mind. *So, we'll be getting a new bishop. That will surely be a change for the better, no matter who is chosen. I wish it would be George. He understands people better than most of the other ministers.*

She thought back to Sylvester's remarks about her brother Adam. *Sylvester could get a lot of benefit from Adam's influence. Adam has always been the kindest of my brothers, and he really wants to do what is right. He and Sylvester are miles apart on what they consider true Christianity to be. But Adam and Jonathan would get along well.*

The next day found them on the road, driving to the viewing. It would be a large event, and Sylvester was anxious not to lose too much time, so they left early. It was a two-hour drive, and long before they got there, little Andrew grew tired of driving.

"Andrew! Stop your whining," his father snapped. Naomi jumped more than Andrew did. Unfortunately, the interruption to his week's schedule hadn't improved Sylvester's patience any. "Bishop Amos was sure an ornery fellow—he chose the most inconvenient week of the summer to die," he grumbled to Naomi. To miss the viewing or the funeral was unthinkable, however. So, like everyone else in the local Mennonite congregations, Sylvester dropped his work and did his duty.

It was only a little after 10:00 in the morning when Sylvester and Naomi arrived at the bishop's home, but already the area was teeming with buggy traffic. Sylvester spat over the side of the buggy.

"We'll be here for hours with this many people," he grunted. "Should have left at 7:00 instead of 8:00."

Despite his bad humor, he wordlessly gave the reins over to one of the hostlers to take care of Star, their faithful horse. He and Naomi joined the lengthy line of people waiting to view the aged bishop's body and shake hands with his family. The air was hot and grew even hotter before it was finally their turn to enter the house an hour and a half later. The body, dressed in a white shroud, lay in a wooden coffin. Custom dictated that they would briefly view the body, saying goodbye to the bishop in their minds. Then they passed on to greet the family, which consisted of the bishop's wife, all their children, all their in-laws, all their grandchildren, and some great-grandchildren.

Even Naomi was glad when they were through with the ordeal. Sylvester stayed polite through the whole episode, but when they were finally on the road home, and away from the crowd, he drew in a deep breath of fresh air.

"I wonder how many of those people were there because they wanted to be." He shook Star's reins impatiently, urging him to move faster. "I don't know anyone who liked the bishop very much. Not even my father."

Naomi remembered her brother's funeral a little too well to say much. She had gotten real comfort from the friends and acquaintances who had taken the time to come and talk to them. But she understood Sylvester's feelings. "It does seem a bit overdone," she agreed. "If he hadn't been the bishop, half of those people wouldn't be there."

The next day was the funeral. "At least the church is only half as far away as the viewing was," Sylvester said as they drove out the lane. "But if we don't get there early we'll have to stand in the sun for the whole service."

He had worked late the night before, catching up, and was feeling a little better than he had the day before.

"At least I'm almost done with that job for the doctor in town," he said. "I promised I'd be finished by Saturday evening. Looks like I might make it." He sounded pleased.

Sylvester tilted his head and looked at the sky to gauge the time. He shook the reins and urged Star to a faster gait. "The bishop should have told me he planned to die this week."

Naomi bit her lip, unsure if the feeling behind his words was genuine. *Your time will come too. Then people will drop their work for your viewing and funeral.* But she knew better than to voice her thoughts. Instead she remarked discreetly, "At least it isn't raining today. That would be a lot worse, especially if we can't get inside the church building."

Their fears proved true. The church wasn't nearly big enough to hold all the people who came. Perhaps a quarter of them, mostly family and visiting ministry, were able to get inside after the burial had taken place. The rest of them stood outside respectfully, and tried to hear as much of the sermon as possible.

The ordination to replace Bishop Amos took place late that fall. A bishop ordination was different from a minister or deacon ordination.[3] Every ordained minister in the district where Amos had been bishop was eligible to be ordained bishop and would "share the lot." Ordinations took place on Thursday, so once again Sylvester and Naomi found themselves traveling to church on a weekday.

This time Naomi and Sylvester both managed to get seats in the building, though many others had to stand outside in the chilly weather. A dozen men sat at the front of the building, facing the

---

[3] The Mennonite Church was never as structured as some denominations are. Each congregation had a lay-preacher and a deacon. It was a lifelong calling. They used the lot to choose these men from a group of men nominated by the congregation from among their membership. The bishop would place a slip of paper in a songbook. He would place this book with other identical books at the front of the church. Each candidate would take a book. The man who chose the book with the paper in it was considered to be God's choice for the office.

The bishop took oversight, often over several congregations, and led out in ceremonies like communion and baptism. He was also responsible to keep order in the congregations. Most Mennonite groups at the time didn't have a written standard, but they had strong expectations of their members. The bishop had a lot of leeway in enforcing his personal ideals on his congregations. But the practice of having semi-annual council services before each communion, tended to be a balancing influence that held the bishop's authority in check. These council services were important, and even the bishop was expected to submit to the voice of the congregation as given in the council service.

preaching table. Several were missing. Sylvester's father and one other minister had asked the bishops to excuse them because of their age. They also excused a younger minister because of lack of experience.

Naomi had a good seat with an excellent view of the proceedings. *I'm glad Sylvester's father isn't sharing the lot,* she thought. *He's been easy to get along with since we're married, but I'd hate to take a chance on upsetting everything. I'm afraid Sylvester would become haughty with the other men if his father were ordained bishop. His family struggles with that already.*

First the congregation sang an old German hymn together. Naomi loved the old German hymns, sung in unison, and so majestic. *And they have such deep meaning,* she thought. *Some of them were written by martyrs and all of them were written by people who really believed what they were saying. I wonder why the church today doesn't have more people like that. It seems we always have to go to sixteenth-century hymns or the* Martyrs Mirror *to see how Christians should live.*

Several visiting bishops took charge of the service. The first bishop was an older man who had come from a distance to help with the ordination. Naomi couldn't help but notice the gravity on his face. *He knows what these men are facing. He's been there. And he knows what a huge responsibility will be given to one of them today.* She listened carefully while he spoke. He preached in German. This wasn't Naomi's mother tongue, but she could understand it well because of years of listening to such sermons.

The speaker took his sermon from the first chapter of Titus. He applied the message to himself rather than to the men in front of him.

That's an interesting way of preaching an ordination sermon. He still realizes how serious his calling is, even though he has been ordained for years. Naomi noticed tears in the speaker's eyes.

"None of us are worthy of such a calling," he told the little group in front of him. "You will only be able to live up to God's standards by humbling yourself under His hand and depending on His help."

These were new words for Naomi. *He preaches like George would. I wonder how some of the ministers are feeling.* She glanced at George and saw that his head was bowed. *He's praying. He understands what this bishop is talking about.*

The ordination came next, before the closing sermon. Naomi could feel the mixture of expectancy and suspense that filled the room. *No wonder. This ordination could influence our district for years, maybe even decades. And it will change the life of one man for sure, and his family too.*

The bishops placed a row of identical books on a little table in front of the preaching table. There was one book for every minister taking part in the lot. One of the books had a slip of paper in it, but even the bishops did not know where it was. No one knew but God.

Naomi gripped the bench she was sitting on. Her knuckles turned white, though she didn't notice. *God, please choose carefully. Please give us the man we need.* Her prayer was no doubt echoed many times throughout the room. The first man got up and took a book. Then the second man. Then the third. Once every man had a book, the bishop stepped around the preaching table to examine their books, one at a time.

The suspense was almost unbearable. Naomi watched closely. *It isn't in that book. Nor in that book. It must be a younger man, because they started at the oldest and are going by age. Not that book either. Now it is George's turn.* The bishop opened the book and stopped.

It's George. He found the paper in George's book. Thank you, Lord.

But George wasn't thanking God at that moment. In fact, she could see his shoulders shaking and realized he was fighting his emotions. Wordlessly, he stood, then answered the questions they asked him—solemn vows that would stay with him for the rest of his life. Then he knelt and the bishops placed their hands on his head. One bishop gave the charge. The other one prayed.

Naomi didn't remember much from the closing sermon by the other visiting bishop. It was probably a good sermon, but she couldn't get her eyes off George's slumped shoulders. *That man has a big job ahead. I think he realizes that the Mennonite church has a lot of needs. We are far from being what our forefathers were. We need help. Oh God, help George to do this. Help him to make a difference.*

Sylvester and Naomi had a quiet ride home, but Naomi's mind was busy. *I wonder what Sylvester is thinking. He always liked George. I've heard him say that George is the only minister he thinks he could ever talk to. If only he would go to George and unload whatever is bothering him. I'm sure George would gladly help him.*

Sylvester didn't speak until they were almost home. "Well, I hope for George's sake that things go well for him," he said tersely. "A lot of our people think he's a liberal. They'll be watching him pretty closely for a while to see what road he takes."

Naomi looked disturbed. "Do you really think there will be trouble? What has he done wrong?"

Sylvester shook his head. "He hasn't done anything wrong, as far as I'm concerned. But too many of the wrong people like him. That makes the older men, like my father, distrust him. I hope he survives it. Some of them will be looking for ways to discredit him."

Naomi was quiet for a little. "It doesn't seem fair. He is such a godly man, and I'm sure he wants the best for our church. How could they do that to him?"

"Maybe I'm wrong," Sylvester said. But the tone of his voice told Naomi that he was sure he wasn't. He continued cautiously. "I overheard several men talking after the service. They were quite upset, and discussing what they could do."

They turned into the lane and Sylvester stopped at the house to let Naomi off. "Better not say much to my parents about the ordination," he cautioned. Naomi could tell he was deciding whether to say more or not. "You see, one of the men I heard talking was my father."

Naomi watched him drive to the wagon shed to unhitch the horse. Her heart sank. Would this turn into another cause of disagreement between her and Sylvester?

Child-Training Problems

13

If you want to alienate your wife, mistreat her children.
It works every time.
—*Bishop George*

Sylvester seemed to love Naomi as much as his personality allowed him to love anyone, except himself. As long as she didn't meddle in his life and did her share of the work, he was happy enough. It took a lot of prayer and grace for Naomi to accept that her husband didn't care much about her inner life. She tended to make up for this lack by pouring her soul into her children.

"Andrew!" Naomi jumped at the harsh bark of Sylvester's voice. She turned just in time to see Sylvester pick up his little son by one arm, give him a swat on the rear that swung the wailing baby through the air, and deposit him in his play pen.

He turned to her, his eyebrows almost meeting over his nose. "Naomi, you need to teach that boy to listen. If he's old enough to walk and talk, he's old enough to stay out of your cupboards."

Naomi cringed under Sylvester's stern look. "He's awfully young to be that strict with," she said timidly. But rather than upset Sylvester more, she added, "I'll try. I don't mind cleaning up a bit after him. Playing with the pots and pans keeps his attention."

To herself she added, *I wonder why he's so paranoid about Andrew's behavior? His nieces and nephews aren't any different than Andrew.*

Sylvester walked to the door. "He's getting old enough to help clean up his toys. He'll end up a lazy ne'er-do-well if we don't get to training him."

Naomi leaned against the kitchen table for support as she watched Sylvester stride across the lane to his shop. She could feel herself trembling. *I know that Sylvester is right,* she admitted to herself. *But I can hardly make myself discipline my little boy. He gets so much of that from his father, and I want him to feel loved by someone. But I must do better or Sylvester will try to do it.*

She did try. She really did. But little Andrew seemed to sense her feelings, and took advantage of her every time she turned her back. Sylvester noticed that as well.

"Naomi, we need to talk about Andrew," he started one evening after supper. He must have seen her cringe, because his voice softened a little. "I know you hate to train him and that it makes you feel mean. But one of these times he's going to hurt himself because he hasn't learned to listen. At lunch time I barely got him stopped from touching the stove. Fortunately, it wasn't very hot this time, but some time it will be, and he'll burn himself."

Naomi sighed. *He's right. I know he is. But how can I do it?* She tried to squelch the rebellious thought and answer in a normal tone of voice. "I know. I saw him." She clasped her hands on the table to try to keep them from trembling. "I'll try to do better. But he always waits until I have my back turned, then takes off. I can hardly get anything done."

"Well," Sylvester replied. "If you can't do it, I'll have to. I know you don't like my child-training methods and I've held back because of it. But I won't have him grow up a spoiled brat."

He dropped the subject, but Naomi knew he meant what he said, and she trembled inside.

"Could you put a large kettle of water on the stove for me?" They had just finished breakfast and Naomi was clearing the dishes off the table. "I'd like to wash up our bedding and winter underwear before I pack them away for the summer."

She stuffed the stove with wood before she started gathering the wash into piles on the kitchen floor. The water was almost boiling by the time she brought in her washtubs and her washboard. But she had forgotten the soap, and dashed to the woodshed to get it.

"EEEEEE!"

She froze, her blood running cold. Where was Andrew? She raced for the kitchen as Andrew let out another blood-curdling shriek. He was standing by the red-hot stove.

Sylvester had heard the scream as well, and came running through the kitchen door. He took in the scene in one glance and grabbed the hysterical little boy and plunged his hand into a tub of cool water that Naomi had intended to use for rinse water.

Sylvester shouted over his shoulder, "Run to the ice house and get some ice. Quick, don't just stand there!"

Naomi shook herself loose and raced out the door, almost falling down the front steps. Behind her, Andrew let out another wail. She ripped open the door of the icehouse and grabbed a chunk of ice buried in the sawdust by the door. She wrapped her apron around it and ran for the house.

"Rinse off the ice and put it in the water," Sylvester ordered. "We've got to stop this burn from getting worse."

Little Andrew's eyes were wide open when his mother reappeared with the ice, but he had stopped crying. Uncontrollable hiccupping sobs shook his small frame.

"Grab the hatchet in the wood box," Sylvester said behind her. "Knock the ice into smaller pieces and put them in the tub to make the water colder. And close the draft on that stove. It's roasting in here."

Blindly, Naomi followed his instructions. She was beyond thinking for herself. But she realized when she turned to the stove that the hot water was boiling and the stove was pouring out heat. She closed the draft completely and heard the roar of flames subside. But the stove pipe was red hot and the flames crackled as they shot up into the chimney.

Sylvester noticed this at the same time. "Run outside and make sure the chimney isn't on fire," he said. "That would be just what we need right now."

The chimney, fortunately, was all right. It had handled the blast of heat without any further harm, likely because Sylvester had plastered it the previous fall. Sylvester nodded tersely as she told him the good news. "Well, it will be cleaned right out after a blast of heat like that," he said. "You could have burned the whole house down with a fire like that in the stove."

Naomi pushed back the hair from her face with trembling hands. Sylvester relented as he saw the tears in her eyes. "Anyhow, all's well that ends well." He pulled Andrew's burned hand from the ice-cold water and looked at it. "You take Andrew and keep his hand in the water until I'm back. I'll run over and get my mother. When it comes to burns, she's better than a doctor."

Naomi was still trembling but she took Andrew from him and sat on the floor beside the wash tub. He fastened his eyes on her, but only whimpered as she pushed his hand back into the water. "That's right, little sweetheart," she whispered. "You be my brave little boy."

About an hour later, Sylvester's mother, Adah, bustled into the door, cackling like a mother hen. Andrew had fallen asleep in Naomi's arms.

"Poor little lamb," she clucked softly. "Let me see that hand." She shook her head as she looked at the burned fingers and palm. "My, oh my," Adah said. "That's a bad one. It's good you thought to put it in ice water to stop it from going deeper."

Naomi dropped her eyes and admitted, "It wasn't me, it was Sylvester. I wouldn't have known what to do, but he must have heard the screaming and came running."

"I was outside getting lumber when he screamed," Sylvester said. "It was the most blood-curdling scream I've heard in a long time. Enough to wake the dead."

Adah shook her head again. "They can move so fast, these little ones. Sylvester did that himself when he was Andrew's age. I just went outside to get some water and he waddled over to the stove. Unfortunately, this one is even worse than what he got."

Naomi looked at Sylvester. "I've still got scars from it," he said, holding out his hand to show her. "It was mostly this finger."

Adah had noticed how shaken Naomi was and stayed to help her do the washing. Naomi was grateful that she didn't ask for a lot of details about Andrew's burn. Despite her loose tongue, Adah could be circumspect when she saw the need. But she did ask about how things were going for her and Sylvester.

"So, Sylvester never told you about his burn?" she asked. "He still remembers it, I think. It was a very traumatic experience for him."

Naomi shook her head. "No, he hasn't," she replied. "I've often wondered what happened to his hand, but he doesn't seem to like personal questions . . ." Her voice trailed off, but Adah caught what she said.

She looked at Naomi carefully. "So, he's still like that, is he?" she asked. "We never really were able to get close to him when he was still at home. I thought surely he would change once he was married."

Naomi shook her head again. "No, and I've never learned how to read him," she admitted shamefacedly. "He won't talk to me about anything personal."

Adah pursed her lips. "His father is the opposite extreme. He's always babbling about his feelings. Gets tiresome sometimes. But," she added thoughtfully, "I think I'd rather have it that way than not knowing how he was feeling or what he was thinking. I'll talk to Simon and see if he would talk to Sylvester."

Naomi wasn't so sure about that. "What if he thinks I was complaining to you about him? He sure wouldn't like that."

Adah pursed her lips again. "Well, let me talk to Simon. Sylvester might listen to his father if he came to talk to him. But I sure don't want to get you in trouble. Is he harsh to you?" Her keen eyes examined her daughter-in-law.

Naomi hardly knew what to say. "He doesn't hit me or anything like that," she said haltingly. "But he has a way of making me feel like a total idiot just by being quiet. If only he would talk to me. We have this horrible barrier between us and I don't know what it is."

Adah looked puzzled. "That's strange. I don't remember him being quite that bad. I will talk to Simon. He might have a better idea how to approach it. It's going to be a long lifetime for you if nothing changes."

It took three long weeks for Andrew's hand to heal. Naomi expected a lecture from Sylvester about child training, but he never brought it up again. His father came over a few days after it happened and had a long talk with Sylvester. Naomi never learned what it was about, and she didn't borrow trouble by asking. But she thought about it a lot.

Sylvester didn't scold me for what happened to Andrew. Nor did he ever say anything about what his father wanted. I wonder if his father talked to him about our relationship. Things have been a little better, though he still won't talk to me about anything in his life. But he has been helping to change the dressings on Andrew's burns. It's amazing how gentle he can be for something like that.

After that, Naomi put her heart and soul into training Andrew. And she made progress, though Sylvester still watched his son critically and felt free to apply discipline whenever he thought it necessary.

Several months later, a new baby joined the family. This time it was a little girl and they called her Martha. Three years later, Hettie was born. By now Andrew was six and quite a little man, at least in Naomi's mind. He had learned to be obedient to a fault. Sylvester kept a black strap in the barn that he used to reinforce his instructions, and Andrew had long since learned to fear it. However, Andrew was only six and sometimes was careless despite his respect for the strap. This upset his father, who was very organized and never forgot anything.

The upheavals troubled Naomi, even though she realized Andrew needed to learn to overcome his carelessness. *I wish I could help Andrew be more careful. He gets so many spankings, and I know he fears his father. He does so much daydreaming and then he forgets what he was told to do. But he is only a six-year-old. I think Sylvester expects too much of him at times.*

Naomi kept talking to Andrew about his problem with absentmindedness, but he couldn't seem to shake the habit completely. One evening, Sylvester had enough. It was a blustery, dark evening and he had given Andrew specific instructions about closing the barn door before supper. Andrew, however, was busy imagining he was deer hunting and forgot all about it. While Sylvester was finishing a few chores after supper, he found the barn door swinging in the wind.

"Andrew!" The boy froze at the sound of his father's voice. He knew very well what that tone meant. Naomi looked up from her work and caught her breath at the look on Sylvester's face.

"Young man," his father barked. "I told you to make sure those barn doors were shut when you came in. And you left them open! You can go out there right now and close them. And hurry up about it."

Andrew's face blanched. Naomi knew how afraid he was of the dark. Just that month a cougar had carried away a little girl, on an evening much like this one. Surely Sylvester wasn't going to send him out there alone.

"But, but . . . " Naomi's voice faltered as she saw the look on Sylvester's face.

"You can stay out of this," he informed her coldly. "Andrew is going to learn right here and now that he needs to do what he is told. This has happened too often."

He turned to Andrew. "And while you're out there, bring the strap in with you."

Andrew's eyes were wide with terror, and Naomi's heart went out to him. "Can . . . Can I go with him?" she asked timidly.

"No! I told you to stay out of this, and I meant that." Sylvester's face was like flint.

Andrew took another look at his father's face, and headed for the door. Naomi could see that he was shaking, and she prayed that God would send an angel to go with him. Time dragged. It was only a few minutes but it seemed much longer until Andrew came back, carrying the strap.

Had quite an episode with Andrew. That boy needs to learn to mind his business. I don't care if he is only six. I had told him specifically to shut the barn door. And he didn't. So I sent him out in the dark to do it. He's scared of the dark, and that ought to teach him a lesson. Then I paddled him, just to help it sink in. I don't want him to grow up to be scatterbrained. I wish Naomi wouldn't take these things so seriously though. She started to cry when I spanked him. And she hasn't talked to me all evening. Well, so be it. Andrew's going to learn, and Naomi can learn at the same time.

It was only the beginning. Naomi's mother-heart yearned for her children, yet she dared not interfere when Sylvester decided it was time to teach one of them a lesson. *If only Sylvester could learn to show some love to us.* Naomi was sitting at the kitchen table, waiting for him to get home from town. *I wonder why he's so late tonight? He is often late for supper when he goes to town, but he's hardly ever this late. The children have been in bed for over half an hour already.*

Her mind rambled on, while she kept one ear tuned to the driveway, listening for Sylvester's horse. *I wish he could see how happy the children can be when he isn't around. But it would probably offend him if he knew. It's strange—he does seem to love them. I overheard him telling his father about a little barn that Andrew made with some scrap lumber. He made it sound as if Andrew was smart for his age and handy with tools. But when Andrew had showed him the barn earlier, he hardly looked at it. Grandpa seems to suspect what is going on. He spends a lot of time with the children when he comes around, and especially with Andrew. Maybe he is trying to give the love to his grandsons now that he never gave his sons.*

Naomi got up from her chair at the table and wandered restlessly around the kitchen. She put a few dishes in the cupboard, and absentmindedly straightened a motto on the wall. She peered out the kitchen window into the deepening twilight. Nothing. She opened the door and listened. Nothing.

She stood there for a moment, undecided, then sat down on the top porch step. *A lot has taken place since the night Sylvester and I first sat on these steps together. I had no idea what married life was going to be like. I just assumed we would have the kind of relationship my parents had, and my brothers have with their wives—by no means perfect, but . . . somehow less lonely than ours.*

Wistfully, she watched the moon come into sight on the horizon.

Where is Sylvester? It was probably the dozenth time she had wondered that tonight. *I should get up and do something while I wait.* But she couldn't drag herself to her feet.

She thought again of that first night when she had sat beside Sylvester on this same step. *If only . . . if only someone had warned me what married life was going to be like.* She leaned against the post and clung to it. She felt the familiar tears coming, running slowly down her cheeks. She started to shake, and sobs wracked her body.

She must have cried herself to sleep because that was how Sylvester found her half an hour later when he finally got home. Her arms were wrapped tightly around the porch post, and her tearstained cheek was pressed against it.

Sylvester pulled his horse to a stop in front of the porch and jumped from his buggy. "Are you okay? Is something wrong?"

Naomi woke with a start, not remembering for a moment where she was. "I was . . . I am . . . I . . . " Her voice trailed off and she shook her head, trying to grasp what was going on. "I was waiting here for you. I guess I must have fallen asleep."

"Apparently." His answer was abrupt. He had seen the tearstains on her cheeks. "You should go to bed. I'll be a few minutes yet. Did you feed the cattle?"

Naomi crawled stiffly to her feet, swaying slightly as she regained her balance. "Yes, I finished the chores."

He turned without further ado and led his horse to the driving shed where he unhitched. She watched him for a moment in the moonlight, then slowly turned and entered the house. She stopped just inside the door, where he couldn't see her.

"He's been drinking," she whispered wretchedly. "I wonder who he was with. But there's no use asking. He'll just say it was a customer."

Naomi has hardly spoken to me since my episode with Andrew. She really took it hard. Maybe I was too hard on him. Andrew will hardly come close to me. Seems scared *of me. I thought he could go to town with me today, but he didn't want to go. I thought if he was along it might help me stay away from places I know I shouldn't go. Sometimes I wish I could be more like other people are. I think if I could make myself tell Naomi about ____, it would change things. But I can't seem to make myself do that.*

Here Today, Gone Tomorrow

14

As for man, his days are as grass: as a flower of the field, so he flourisheth. For the wind passeth over it, and it is gone; and the place thereof shall know it no more (Psalm 103:15-16).

It was a beautiful day in mid-May. Sylvester had piled Naomi and his three children into the buggy and taken them to church. Naomi was holding Hettie, and Andrew was squeezed between Naomi and Sylvester. Martha was partly on Andrew's lap and partly on Naomi's.

"I'm going to have to buy a two-seater buggy," Sylvester remarked as they left church for home.

"Andrew, move over!" His voice sharpened as Andrew squirmed and twisted, trying to find more room. "And stop wriggling."

Naomi moved over as much as she could to give Andrew more room, before replying to Sylvester's first comment. "Another baby would pretty well make us overflow this buggy."

Sylvester stiffened a little. "I'm not sure we can afford another baby right now. A boy wouldn't be so bad, because he would bring in a little income. But girls mostly cost you, and you still need to give them a good start in life."

Naomi raised her eyebrows a little at this, but didn't reply, at least not audibly. *So they're just a liability unless they can pay for themselves by bringing in enough income. I wonder if he feels that way about me too?*

But rather than adding fuel to the fire, she changed the subject. "I wonder what Bishop George meant by what he said about using tobacco and drinking hard cider." She shifted a little so that she could see Sylvester better. "He didn't seem to leave much room for it."

Sylvester grunted. "I don't think that went down very well. Even the conservatives in the church don't want to give up their cigars and chewing tobacco.[1] And everyone likes a glass of cool cider during the hot summer."

He shook the reins to urge the horse to a faster trot. "I told you, he'd better be careful. I like George better than most of the other preachers, but he is going to lose his support pretty quickly if he isn't careful."

He glanced over his shoulder as if to make sure no one was following close enough to overhear their discussion. "My pop is one of the preachers, and he drinks some hard cider occasionally. I've never seen him smoke a cigar, but I know he keeps a tin of chewing tobacco in his shop. I'm guessing most married men chew occasionally."

Naomi knew Sylvester had several tins of chewing tobacco in his shop too. And she knew he stopped in town for a few glasses of cider occasionally, though she still hadn't figured out who he shared them with.

She remembered her brothers having a similar discussion. "My brother Adam feels the same way George does," she said timidly. "He doesn't drink or chew."

Sylvester snorted in disgust. "That's a Methodist for you. They

---

[1] In many cases it was the church's "conservatives" who held on to these things. People who wanted to change, even to have healthier morals, were generally considered "liberals" who were candidates to leave for the Methodists or Dunkards.

think they will go to heaven because they are so much better than the rest of us."

"I don't think Adam feels that way," Naomi protested. "In fact, I've heard him say you won't go to heaven because of your good works."

Sylvester backed up a bit. "Well, I guess he isn't as bad as some. But some of those Methodists, and Dunkards too, are pretty uppity about their Christianity. Jesus drank wine; the Bible says He did. My pop always said what was good enough for Jesus is good enough for him."

It was Naomi's turn to squirm a little now. "I guess I don't know enough about the Bible to say who is right. Maybe you should talk to George and ask him about it. He was pretty careful with what he said, so he didn't really explain why he felt that way."

Sylvester grunted again. "He had better be careful," he replied. "He could still find himself put out of the church or silenced. I know things have quieted down a lot, but too many sermons like this one will stir everything up again. Andrew! Sit still!"

That ended the conversation for the moment. But Naomi continued to think about it. *I think Bishop George surely has some good reasons for feeling as he does. But I think Sylvester is right. It will take a lot of teaching to get those things out of the church, and I doubt he can do it in this generation. But maybe the next one will look at it differently.*

That conversation came back to haunt Naomi about half a year later. *What will Sylvester say if I tell him we're going to have another baby? He said he would be okay with a boy. I guess I should just tell him and get it over with.*

Sylvester didn't say much. "Hopefully it will be a boy." He shrugged his shoulders. "Girls aren't a lot of use in the shop, but at least a boy could help me for a few years before he works away from home."

"Well, there is not a lot I can do about it," Naomi told him. "God will make that choice, not I." As an afterthought, she added, "Nor will you."

Sylvester just grunted and headed out the door to his shop, as he always did when a subject became too uncomfortable.

Naomi watched him through the window. *Well, that wasn't too bad, I guess. Though I wish he would be happier about it. I wish I could shake him loose from his black moods for once and see him get excited about something.*

Something wasn't right. Naomi got the first inkling of it about a month before the baby was due. "Sylvester, could you get your mother to stop by?" Sylvester's head jerked up and he laid down his spoon. His mother was the local midwife and he hadn't expected this request for a while yet.

Naomi looked pale. "I'm not sure what is happening, but I'd like for her to have a look at me. I know it is early, and maybe it is nothing, but I don't want to take a chance."

She could tell that Sylvester was concerned because he didn't finish his meal, something that hardly ever happened. He didn't say anything, but he pushed his half empty plate aside and jumped to his feet. "I will be back in half an hour," he said, stopping at the door to lace up his boots. A few minutes later, she heard his horse gallop out the lane.

Sylvester's parents both came, and his father took the children over to Naomi's parents for the afternoon. Sylvester, looking haggard, hung around the kitchen until his mother sent him packing.

"Sylvester, there is absolutely nothing you can do to help by walking circles around the kitchen table," Adah told him. "Time will go faster if you get out and do some work."

Sylvester sheepishly took her advice but didn't get much done in his shop either. Several hours later his mother came out to the shop to find him. "Sylvester, I think you'd better run into town and see if you can get the doctor to come out this evening. I think we're going to need him."

Sylvester's horse galloped out the lane for the second time that day. He trained all his horses for riding, because they were worth more that way, though he seldom rode them to town. But when he was in a hurry, it was faster to throw on a saddle and ride than it was to harness the horse and hitch him to a buggy.

And right now, Sylvester was in a hurry.

The doctor got there several hours later. Sylvester had returned an hour before with the news that the doctor would come as soon as he finished looking after the two patients in his office. His father, Simon, returned around the same time.

"Naomi's parents decided they would just keep the children overnight," Simon updated Sylvester and Adah. He looked at Adah. "Are you staying here for the night? If you are, I might as well head home and get myself a bit of supper."

"The doctor will be here soon," Adah replied. "But I won't go home until this is over. Naomi will need my help, regardless of how things turn out."

Simon looked at Sylvester. "Want to come with me?" he asked. "I'm not the best cook in the world, but I can fry up some eggs and potatoes."

Sylvester shook his head. "I'm not hungry." He tugged a chair out from the table and sat down. "I'm not going anywhere until that doctor says everything is okay. Not even out to the shop." He looked at his mother out of the corner of his eye.

That Adah didn't notice what he said was proof of just how worried she was. "I need to get back to Naomi," she said. "Bring the doctor in when he gets here."

She stopped at the bedroom door. "Did you want to see Naomi?" she asked. "I'm sure she would like to see you for a minute or two."

Naomi had never seen Sylvester so sober. Like usual, when things got serious, he didn't know what to say, but he did take Naomi's hand when she reached out to him.

She gave him a half smile. "Hi," she whispered faintly.

He squeezed her hand. "I hope things will be okay," he said. "The children are at your parents' house. And the doctor is on his way." She could tell he didn't know what else to say.

Suddenly Naomi gritted her teeth, and beads of sweat ran down her cheeks.

Adah gently wiped her face with a damp towel. "Just hang in there, dearie," she said. "Everything will be okay. You'll see."

Sylvester slipped out and shut the door behind him. Neither of the two women noticed him leave.

People under stress do strange things. Sylvester went back to walking circles around the kitchen table, counting the number of rounds under his breath. He was just beginning his thirty-fifth round when he heard the doctor drive in.

Sylvester met the doctor and his wife on the front porch. "I brought my wife," the doctor explained. "She's a trained nurse, and I'll probably need her help. Your mother is the best midwife I've ever seen. If she calls for my help, I know things are serious."

He went to the sink. "Have you got some hot water? We need to scrub up before we start."

Sylvester snapped out of his trance and dipped some hot water from the reservoir in the wood stove.

"Keep lots of hot water ready," the doctor said. "We might need it."

Adah heard the voices in the kitchen and came out to see who was there. She sighed with relief when she saw the doctor. "I'm glad to see you," she said. "I've done everything I know at least twice, to no avail. I'm not sure how much more of this she can handle." Her voice lowered and she glanced at Sylvester.

The doctor nodded briskly. "Let's have a look," he said. "These cases can turn around quickly sometimes. Or, they can . . ." He left the sentence hanging in the air.

Adah came for hot water several times during the evening and night. Around midnight, she made some tea for all of them. Sylvester hardly tasted his, but the warmth felt good inside him.

The doctor drank his slowly, and asked for a second cup. "This hits the spot," he said gratefully.

He looked at Sylvester. "I think we're making some progress," he said kindly. "But it could be a long night. You might want to lie down for a while. Maybe in the parlor? We will come and get you if anything changes."

Unfortunately, it was early morning before anything changed. Naomi would look back at that night as the worst night of her life. Except for the constant pain, she didn't really remember much of it. She wasn't quite sure, looking back on it later, but she thought she might have even prayed that she could die.

She never did find out how Sylvester felt or how he spent the night.

Baby Eli was born about 4:30 that morning, and even the doctor was relieved when it was all over. Adah was ecstatic and ran to tell Sylvester. Naomi was beyond feeling. Never in her life had she felt so tired and weak.

The doctor had little time to spend with her. He saw at a glance that it would be a miracle if the baby survived, and leaving Naomi in Adah's capable hands, he employed every available strategy to save the little boy's life.

Naomi wasn't sure where Sylvester came from, but suddenly he was at her side. "Well, you've got your little boy," she whispered. "Let's call him Eli, after your grandpa."

Adah didn't leave them alone for long. She came bustling back in. "Now we've got to let Naomi sleep," she said. "You come out here, into the kitchen, Sylvester. I'll make some more tea."

The doctor looked up from the little baby. "Make me a cup too, please," he said wearily. "This fight isn't over yet."

For the first time, Naomi realized that she hadn't even seen her baby. "Is he . . . okay?" Her voice trembled. "When can I hold him?"

Her mother-in-law patted her hand gently. "The doctor is looking after him," she soothed. "You need to get some sleep so you can look after him later." Naomi noticed Adah brushed a tear from the corner of her eye, but she was too worn out to figure out why.

The last thing she heard as she drifted off to sleep was the doctor telling Adah, "Get a basket ready to use for a bed. Warm it up thoroughly in the oven. He is going to need 24-hour care for a while."

Naomi had a little boy this morning. Born early, and she had a tough time. A really tough time. I thought for sure she was going to die. I really wished I could talk to her long enough to ask her to forgive me for a few things. But she was too far gone, and the doctor was right there all the time. It was a real relief when she finally had the baby. Called him Eli, after my grandpa. Well, I got my boy. Hope he's okay after the tough time he had.

The doctor left right after breakfast to attend another baby case. His wife bunked down in the children's bedroom for a few hours of rest while Adah looked after Naomi and the baby. Sylvester spent his morning in the shop.

Adah brought Baby Eli to Naomi about mid-morning, when Naomi woke up.

"He's so little," Naomi gasped. "I've never seen such a tiny baby!"

"He'll need a lot of care," Adah said gently. "It'll take a few weeks to get him off to a good start."

Naomi didn't comment, but her heart sank. *Oh, no; he'll never make it, but no one wants to tell me. Poor Sylvester, he wanted a boy so bad, now this.* She cuddled Eli close and he whimpered a bit. *Poor little boy. It's not his fault. I hope he isn't suffering.*

Everyone tried hard. Even Sylvester took his turn caring for Eli. But it was a losing battle from the very start. The next day, as Naomi was holding him, little Eli breathed his last. Sylvester was with her. When he saw it was over, he stumbled into the kitchen to get his mother. Then he fled outside.

The rest of the day was a blur for Naomi. Gentle hands took the baby from her. The nurse gave the heartbroken mother a sleeping draught so she could rest, but she woke up six hours later trying to find her baby. Finally, night came, then morning. Sylvester brought the baby to her bedside so she could see him one more time. He had stayed up late the night before making a little coffin for his son. He refused any offers for help.

Neighbors slipped in and out as word spread, and Bishop George and his wife came to pray with Naomi and Sylvester. Through it all, Naomi was so numb she hardly knew what people said or did.

That afternoon they took the little coffin with its precious bundle to the graveyard where a few kind friends had dug the grave that morning. Naomi, still weak from the birth, stayed behind with her mother, but later Adah told her about the service.

It was only a graveside service. But Bishop George and his wife had once lost a little one. He knew how it felt, and everyone who heard his prayer that day knew he understood their grief. Then Sylvester helped to fill in the grave.

When it was all over, members of both sides of the family as well as Bishop George and his wife returned to the house with Sylvester. Here George led another little service for Naomi's sake.

We buried Eli today. Naomi is heartbroken. I am too, I guess. I had big plans for Eli. Wonder if God is punishing me. Too bad he had to punish Naomi along with me. It's really tough on her. I talked to Bishop George for a while. He sure is a kind person. I really felt like pouring everything out to him, but somehow, I couldn't make myself.

It took a few weeks for Naomi to feel anywhere close to normal. She still burst into tears at the slightest provocation, but things gradually improved for her. Sylvester was amazingly gentle with her, but very quiet.

One evening, after the children were in bed, they sat on the porch steps and watched the sun setting. Naomi slipped over close to Sylvester. He stared at the horizon for a long time before turning to look at her. She caught her breath at the tortured look in his eyes.

"Sylvester, what's wrong?" She took his hand in both of hers. "Why can't you tell me what you're feeling? I can see you're crying inside."

He looked away, then back at her. "I don't know. God is punishing me, I guess. But I wish He wouldn't punish you, too."

It was the most he had ever said about his feelings. But she could see his barriers were already going back up. He slapped his hands on his thighs and got to his feet. "We'd better get to bed," he said briskly. "You still need to make sure and get your sleep. I need to check the cattle then I'll be in."

Naomi watched him walk to the barn. *He came so close. If only he would have let go. I wonder if I'll ever know what is holding him away from me.*

Almost spilled everything to Naomi tonight. I'm not sure why I didn't, except she's already hurting so bad, I didn't want to add to it. Not sure which would hurt her worse, my telling her the truth, or hiding it. I think she knows there is something. If only I weren't so stubborn. Can't seem to help it.

Naomi's God 15

Hardships often prepare ordinary people for an extraordinary destiny.
—C. S. Lewis

Later, Naomi would look back at the loss of her youngest child as a turning point in her life. While she had always tended to have a spiritual perspective of life, losing her baby drove her to her knees with a renewed desperation for God. He honored her pursuit by helping her find a deeper inner peace that only He can give.

It seemed different for Sylvester. He watched Naomi, but didn't join her in her search. Instead he seemed to withdraw even further into himself.

Sylvester frowned when he noticed that Naomi was holding their old German family Bible in her lap. "That Bible belonged to my grandmother," he said curtly. "I'd hate to see it worn out or spoiled."

Naomi closed the Bible carefully. "I know," she replied softly. "But it's the only one we have."

"The preachers read the Bible to us on Sundays," Sylvester pointed out. "That seems to be enough for most people."

"But that's only once a month, a lot of the time," Naomi protested. "Ever since Baby Eli was taken from us, I have this deep longing in my heart to know more about God. Church is fine, but it isn't enough."

She brushed a tear from the corner of her eye. She carefully laid the Bible on the old corner cupboard where they kept it, and joined Sylvester at the table for lunch with the children.

Other than scolding Andrew for not cleaning up his plate, Sylvester was quiet for most of the meal. But he continued their conversation as he scraped up his last bite of applesauce. "I think they have some smaller German Bibles in the general store in town," he told Naomi offhandedly. "I could check and see if they have one for a decent price."

Naomi's face lit up. "Oh, would you? I would so love to have a Bible of my own." She didn't smile much these days. But the thought of having her own Bible made her forget her sorrow for the moment.

"Well, I was thinking of going to town anyway, sometime soon. Maybe I'll go this afternoon and see if I can find you one." Sylvester slipped out the door and was gone before Naomi could respond to this unusual remark.

But she had much to think about that afternoon. *Sylvester is different since the baby died. He would never have spent money on a Bible before. He didn't even make a fuss about the cost like he usually would. I hope they have a German Bible. He'll never buy an English one, and I'm not very good at reading English anyway.*

As usual, Sylvester was very quiet when he returned from town. He seemed preoccupied with something, but he did drop a package on the table. "It was the only one they had," he said. "I was going to get a smaller one, but they would have had to order it in. And it would have cost just as much as this one."

He vanished into the parlor after supper while Naomi tucked the children into bed. After she finished cleaning up the kitchen and putting the dishes and leftover food away, she finally sat down at the table to open her parcel. She glanced longingly at the door to the parlor, but as usual it was closed. *I wish Sylvester would take time to look at my new Bible with me. But he always seems too embarrassed or awkward to show his emotions.*

But she forgot her thoughts as she opened the Bible. *My very own Bible! And it's small enough to hold properly while I read.*

Naomi woke with a start, wondering where she was. Then she realized she must have fallen asleep at the table. She carefully closed her Bible before she noticed that Sylvester was standing in the doorway to the parlor. *I must have woke up when he opened the door. I wonder how long he's been standing there watching me. Why doesn't he say something?*

Sylvester watched her put the new Bible beside the family Bible in the corner cupboard. Slowly and deliberately, he spoke, "So, is it what you wanted?"

Naomi smiled. "Yes, it is. Thanks for getting it for me." Impulsively, she gave him a quick hug, something she hadn't done for longer than she cared to remember. At that moment, she was too tired to think of anything but bed, but later she would remember the look in his eyes. She would also remember that he hadn't stiffened as he normally did when she showed her emotions.

He didn't respond directly to her comment or the hug. "You'd better come to bed," he said quietly. "It's getting late, and you've been really tired ever since the baby . . ." His voice trailed off into silence.

She knew he was right. She had been different in many ways since the loss. *I wonder if life will ever be normal again. I'm sure Sylvester won't want to take a chance on going through another episode like that. And I'm not sure I would either. I had no idea losing a baby was like this.*

Got Naomi a Bible today. She has been reading some in Grandmother's old family Bible. That one has been in our family for over a hundred years. My father would have a fit to see it being used regularly. But she seems to get some comfort from reading it, so I thought I'd better get her one for her own. Hate to spend the money. But I owe her something for the way things have been going. Wonder if God thinks He can punish me by punishing her.

It was very late when Naomi woke the next morning. She shook herself, trying to clear the fog from her brain. Then she heard children talking in the kitchen and turned to look at the bedroom clock. That brought her straight up in bed—she could hardly believe her eyes. Never before had she been in bed this late.

Sylvester's side of the bed was empty. He must have decided to let her sleep. *I wonder if he made his own breakfast or went without.* She quickly dressed and brushed her hair back with her fingers. She would have to comb it later.

The children gathered around her as she entered the kitchen. "Father told us not to wake you because you weren't feeling well last night," Andrew informed her. "He warmed up some mush for us."

Naomi's eyes flew to the table. Sure enough, there were the dirty dishes. *How did I ever sleep through all of that? And why didn't Sylvester wake me?*

She sat on the old wooden rocker and pulled the two girls onto her lap, cuddling them close. Andrew leaned on the rocker's arm and looked up into her eyes. "Are you feeling better now? Father said you'd probably feel better if you slept until you woke up by yourself."

Naomi smiled down into his worried eyes. "Yes, I feel a lot better," she assured him. "It was nice of all of you to let me sleep." She watched affectionately as Andrew and Martha ran off to resume their game in the corner. Hettie dropped off to sleep in her arms, so Naomi laid her on the daybed. Looking around, she noticed some hot water on the stove and decided to have a cup of tea. Adah had refilled her container with freshly-dried tea leaves recently.

This is so relaxing. She breathed in the aroma of fresh mint tea. *I think I have enough time to read a little before I make lunch. Funny how I dropped off at the table last night when I was reading. Sylvester must have been afraid something was wrong. I know I've been pretty blue the last while. But I feel better this morning. Though it's not so much the sleep. It's more knowing that he cared enough to let me sleep.*

She opened her Bible to the book of Matthew, where she had been reading the evening before. "Come unto me, all ye that labour and are heavy laden, and I will give you rest."[1] It was like a drink of fresh cold water for her thirsty soul. *I wonder why we don't hear this verse more often in church. It is such a wonderful verse. It is exactly what I need this morning. I have been so tired for so long.*

She read the verse again, then went back to the beginning and read the whole chapter slowly, so it could soak in. *God, you are so good to me. Help me to take your yoke and let you help me with the burden life puts on my shoulders.*

Regretfully, she closed the Bible. She knew already that the book was going to be a close friend. But it was almost lunchtime; she needed to comb her hair, take care of the dirty breakfast dishes, and put together lunch for her little family. *But I actually feel like doing it for a change, Lord. Thank you!*

Sylvester would have had to be blind to miss the change in Naomi when he came in for lunch. He had probably wondered if he would need to make lunch for everyone, but he was greeted by the smell of potato soup bubbling merrily on the stove, and a cup of fresh hot tea by his plate. No sign remained of the breakfast dishes, and the children were playing happily.

In fact, Andrew came bouncing over to greet him. "We let Mama sleep just like you told us to. And she does feel better, like you said she would!"

Sylvester smiled his rare smile and tousled his hair, then glanced at Naomi.

---

[1] In German it gives the idea of "I will refresh you."

She smiled too, and said, "I'll have lunch on the table in a minute. It should be ready by the time you have washed up."

Sylvester had again hired a maid after Eli's birth, but since her three weeks were up, the work had fallen onto Naomi's shoulders again. Sylvester watched for a few moments as she started clearing the lunch dishes, then cleared his throat.

"Make sure you take a nap when the children take theirs," he said. "And don't do more than you need to. My mother is going to stop by tomorrow, and again later in the week to help. She said she would come a couple days a week for now."

He slipped on his boots. "Andrew, you children help your mother, and don't make a big mess around here."

It was hard for Naomi to take a nap when she saw work staring at her from every direction. But she knew Sylvester meant well. And she was already tired, even though she had been up for only three or four hours. *I guess I had better listen to him. I'm glad the garden work is all taken care of for now. I'd hate to see Sylvester's mother needing to look after that as well as her own garden.*

Naomi made another cup of tea, and sat down while she sipped it. *I love hot tea. It's so comforting, somehow.* She opened her Bible again to Matthew 11, and wistfully reread the wonderful invitation at the end of the chapter. *I wish I could have met Jesus. I would have loved to sit at His feet like Mary did and listen to Him. I wonder where that story is.*

She flipped through the rest of Matthew, and then Mark. Finally, in Luke, she found it. She smiled as she read the short account of Mary sitting at Jesus' feet while Martha did the work. *I think I would have acted like Martha. I would have wanted to serve a delicious meal to this famous teacher too.* But she knew that her heart was really with Mary. Down inside, she felt a void—a deep hollow crying out to be filled. Somehow, she knew that Mary had felt a similar void, and Jesus had filled it. *I can't sit at His feet and listen to Him speak. But I* can read the Gospels and hear Him that way.

Naomi closed her Bible carefully and put it in the cupboard. Then she curled up on the day bed. *I'll just take a quick nap here in the kitchen. I've got too much to do to spend all afternoon sleeping.* She turned over in her mind the account she had just read. *I want to be like Mary, not Martha. Mary found her answer, I think. I know I can find mine, too.*

She dropped into a deep, peaceful sleep.

Naomi woke up several hours later feeling that someone was watching her. Sure enough, Andrew was standing beside the day bed, looking at her with large worried eyes. He smiled when he saw that she noticed him.

"Are you awake, Mom?" he asked eagerly, as if he had wanted her to wake up for a while. "You were sleeping for a long time."

Naomi stretched, then reached over and gave him a quick squeeze. "Are the girls still napping?" They were. "Just play quietly until they wake up," she instructed her son. "I'm going to rest a little more." She watched him scamper off. *That nap felt so good. Maybe I have been pushing myself too hard. But I had to do something to keep my mind occupied. Otherwise, I would go crazy thinking about my baby.*

She pushed the thought aside as quickly as it came and thought about Mary and Martha again. *I wonder what became of them. Why weren't they married?*

She watched Andrew construct a wobbly tower out of his favorite wooden blocks. *It must have been a bit hard for Martha to take. She had worked so hard to make a delicious meal for Jesus. But I think Jesus could scold someone without hurting them. He cared so much for them, they couldn't help but respect Him anyway.*

Her mind rambled. *I hope I can go to church on Sunday.* She had missed church the previous two Sundays, and it seemed like an eternity since she had last attended. *When we have church only once a month, missing a service really puts a gap into my life. I wish Bishop George and his wife would stop in again. I wish Sylvester would talk to George about whatever it is that troubles him. I wish, I wish . . .*

She rolled her eyes. *I've got to get up and do something worthwhile before the afternoon is over. At the rate I'm going I'll soon be dreaming my whole day away.* She rolled over and pulled herself to her feet. The room grew blurry and she swayed, then sat down again. *Whoa! I guess I'd better take that a little slower. Sylvester wouldn't be very happy to come in and find me lying on the floor.*

Naomi continued to find solace in her Bible. She started in the beginning of Matthew and read through all four Gospels and Acts. She soon noticed that it helped to take notes as she read. So she asked Sylvester to pick up a cheap notebook and some pencils in town for her. "I'd like to make some notes as I read," she explained. "Sometimes I forget what I've read and where I read it, and I want to be able to write down my thoughts about it. That way I can find the place again."

Sylvester didn't comment, and she wondered what he was thinking. *He seems surprised. But I want to learn more. I don't want to scribble in my Bible. It's probably the only one I will ever own.*

Sylvester brought several small notebooks made from cheap rough paper, and half a dozen pencils. "They've got some of those newfangled rubbers for erasing mistakes," he said. "But I figured you probably wouldn't need them. My mother always used stale bread crusts to erase mistakes."

Naomi smiled, delighted with the notebooks. "These will be fine for what I want. No one will ever read this but me anyway."

That evening, after the dishes were done and the children tucked into bed, Naomi sat down at the table with her Bible and sharpened her pencil with a paring knife. Soon she was deep into the Sermon on the Mount.

She paused, the end of her pencil between her lips as she contemplated. *Keeping notes does slow me down,* she realized. *But it also helps me to understand it better. I guess it forces me to think things through if I write them down.*

Sylvester came in from some last-minute work in his shop. He saw what she was doing and stopped to look over her shoulder. "So, you like writing?" He said it lightly, but the question seemed to have an undertone—a question beyond the question.

She laid down her pencil and turned to look up into his face. His expression was inscrutable, partly shaded in the dim light of the flickering oil lamp.

"Yes, I do," she said slowly, searching his eyes. "It helps me understand what I'm reading." She turned back to her Bible. "See here, in Matthew 6:25. I never noticed before what it says—'*Sorget nicht für euer Leben, was ihr essen und trinken werdet.*' ('Take no thought for your life, what ye shall eat, or what ye shall drink.') I was trying to put that into my own words. Jesus wasn't telling people to be careless about looking after their needs. He was telling them not to be anxious; '*sorget nicht.*' "

Sylvester seemed noncommittal, but he nodded briefly. "Got some bookkeeping to do," he said, and vanished into the parlor, shutting the door behind him.

Naomi watched him go, a bemused look on her face. *Well, so much for that discussion. I wish we could sit and read the Bible together. Many of these teachings are so practical, yet we don't really notice what they are saying.*

The incident, minor though it was, took the heart out of her. She couldn't get her thoughts together again. Closing her Bible, Naomi gathered up her notebook and pencil and carefully placed everything in the cupboard.

She glanced at the closed parlor door, the door that signified everything that was wrong with their marriage. It loomed as an insurmountable barrier between Naomi and her husband. For a wild moment she entertained the thought of smashing her way into the parlor with the axe Sylvester kept in the woodshed. She rolled her eyes and yawned. *I'd better go to bed before I do something stupid. I'm tired. I don't know where that thought came from.*

But as she got ready for bed, she continued pondering the closed parlor door. She remembered hearing a minister say at a wedding that a husband and wife should never hide things from each other. The more she thought of it, the more certain she was that the parlor door was the biggest problem in their home. *No matter what Sylvester is doing or has done, that door is worse. With God's help, we could deal with everything else, no matter how bad it was. But as long as that door is closed between us, nothing will work.*

Teenagers 16

Youth comes but once in a lifetime.
—Longfellow

Sylvester didn't notice his daughters much. He seemed to feel they were Naomi's responsibility. But Andrew's actions he saw as a direct reflection on himself. He intended to raise his son to be an honor to the family name. Unfortunately, he didn't remember what it was like to be young.

It started with school.

Naomi made sure Andrew had everything he needed. "Now be sure to be good, and do what the teacher tells you," she told him. "And play nicely with the other children at recess."

Andrew was almost dancing at the doorway, waiting for his mother to finish her parting speech. He wasn't worried, even if she was. He knew these children, and he had met his teacher, Miss McKee, last week.

Naomi smiled at his eagerness to get going. "Well, walk to the end of the lane, if you wish," she finally relented. "But wait for the Williams children before going any farther. And remember, Susie will show you where to go and what to do when you get to school. Be sure to listen to her."

She wasn't sure how many of these parting admonitions Andrew really heard. He had started off as soon as he heard the word *walk*.

Naomi stood at the door and watched Andrew trot down the lane. Several neighbor children soon arrived and invited him along. Everyone was excited. *I remember how excited we used to be for the first day of school. And I know Susie will make sure that he gets off to a good start. I'm glad he knows her so well. Sylvester doesn't think it is necessary to walk with him, but he seems so little to be going to school, even if he is eight years old.*

Andrew loved learning to read. In no time, he was reading any book he could get his hands on. It became a common chorus. "Andrew, put that book down and help with the dishes." Or, "Andrew, put that book down and go gather the eggs before supper."

Naomi was glad to see him learning to read. Sylvester, however, thought things were going a little overboard.

"Andrew! Put that book away, right now! It's supper time." Sylvester's voice, always a lot sharper than Naomi's, made her cringe. Andrew would jump and come running. But more than once, Andrew forgot his chores because his mind was still in the book he'd been reading. Sylvester finally put his foot down.

"Andrew! Put your book in the cupboard, right now. No more reading this week. You need to learn to do your work without being told all the time." This punishment horrified Andrew, but he knew his father meant it. After that he was more careful and things went better.

One night after supper, Naomi was helping Andrew with his homework. Sylvester was sitting at the table, drinking a cup of tea and listening while Andrew practiced his oral reading and elocution, the gestures and poses that went along with the words.

Sylvester frowned. "Is everything in English at that school? When are you going to learn to read German?"

"Everything is in English," Andrew said. "Our teacher doesn't like German. She says it is an old-fashioned language that people should stop using."

Sylvester's eyes sparked. "Old-fashioned, indeed! German is God's language. The devil gave us English." He pounded his fist on the table for emphasis. "Don't you ever let me catch you reading the English Bible," he thundered.

"But, Father," Andrew objected timidly, "some of our reading passages are from the English Bible, and I would get thrashed if I refused to read them at school."

Sylvester's lips tightened, but he finally relented. Teachers were highly respected in the community, and even Sylvester wouldn't have forced his children to disobey them.[1] "Well, read them at school if you must," he said grimly. "But don't let me catch you reading them at home. The German Bible was good enough for our ancestors and it's good enough for us."

Sylvester's wrath boiled over a year later when his son brought home an English New Testament. Andrew was showing it to Naomi when Sylvester happened to come in the door. "What do you have there?" Sylvester's eyebrows almost met over his nose.

Andrew looked like a cornered rabbit facing a fox. "It's . . . well, it's a New Testament," he stammered. "The school is giving them to the students who finish the second reader."

Sylvester stalked over to Naomi and Andrew. "Let me see it," he demanded, tight lipped. He took it from Andrew and opened it. "Sure enough, it's English." His jaw clenched. "I will not have a Bible written in the devil's language in my house!"

---

[1] The fight between English and German plagued the Mennonite Church for many decades.

He turned to the woodstove, but Naomi protested. "Sylvester! That is a Bible! Won't God curse us for burning His holy word?" She grabbed his arm, an action so abnormal for her that Sylvester stopped short for a moment. Then he pushed her away roughly.

"I said I will not have an English Bible in my house, and I meant it. No book written in English has ever been holy." His words were laced with steel, and Naomi caught her balance and backed away. Andrew's eyes widened, his mouth hanging open as he watched his father march to the stove, open the lid, and throw his precious book into the flames.

The room was quiet, deathly quiet. Sylvester looked from face to frightened face, first at Naomi and Andrew, then at his two daughters. He saw the fear and horror in their eyes. He turned from them and walked out the door to his shop. It was his refuge and no one would bother him there.

Naomi's heart sank as she watched him go, groping blindly for the table to support her trembling form. *Our children will never forget this evening. He has no idea what kind of damage he just did to them. Oh, Sylvester!*

Naomi herself was actually more comfortable with German than English. Her schooling had taken place during the last few years the schools in the area were operated by the church. Then the government-sponsored public schools had taken over. But she had never had the abhorrence of English that Sylvester's family had.

She worried most about Andrew. *He had been so happy with his little testament. And he hardly has any books of his own except for his school books. I wonder if he will ever forgive Sylvester for this.*

Sometimes I think our church families should go back to educating our children at home. Andrew brought home an English New Testament today, of all things. God doesn't speak the devil's language, and I burned it. Naomi didn't like that. She thought I was desecrating

God's word by burning a Bible, but an English Bible isn't
a true Bible. My pop sure would have been upset if I had
let Andrew keep it and read it. A man has a responsibil-
ity to keep up standards in his own home.

The friction between Sylvester and Andrew didn't end when Andrew finished common school. He was a good student, and though he attended longer than most, he wanted to continue his learning. He even harbored a secret desire to attend normal school and become a teacher.[2] Naomi sympathized with him, but she knew that Sylvester, who was anxious for Andrew to begin helping in the woodworking shop, would never consider the investment.

Miss McKee had taught Andrew for all his school years, but she had never stopped in to visit his home. When she came to see Sylvester and Naomi one evening, they knew something was on her mind. They sat around the table and Naomi poured a cup of tea for each of them. Sylvester remained aloof, as usual. He suspected what the teacher wanted and he didn't like women who interfered with his plans.

Miss McKee had experience in dealing with parents, however, and opened the discussion briskly. "I'd like to talk about Andrew's future a little," she said. "He's one of the best students I've ever had, and it seems a shame for him to drop out of school to become a farm laborer or carpenter's helper."

Naomi glanced at Sylvester worriedly. His eyebrows were starting to draw together. Miss McKee must have noticed that danger sign as well because she gave Sylvester her sweetest smile. "He probably takes after you, sir. I've heard you are a good business man."

Sylvester grunted, but didn't say anything, so Miss McKee contin-ued. "Andrew has a lot of potential. I think he would benefit from attending the normal school in the city. That would open the door

---

[2] A normal school was a preparatory school for teaching or further education, comparable to a college.

for him to become a teacher, for instance."

Sylvester grunted again. "So, teachers make more money than farmers or woodworkers?" He sounded dubious. "I haven't seen you getting any fancy wages."

Miss McKee backpedaled a little. "Well, at the beginning he probably wouldn't make as much as that. But with a little experience he would be able to get in with a bigger school and become a principal. If he worked at it, he could eventually teach in a normal school or academy."

"Seems like a lot of ifs and buts to me," was Sylvester's snide remark. "How many years have you taught?"

"About fifteen years," Miss McKee replied. "I'm a woman, and it is unlikely I will be able to advance to that level. But Andrew is a boy. He is one of the best students I've ever had."

Naomi took advantage of a gap in the conversation to fill everyone's tea cups. Then the teacher continued. "I would think that any father would want to see his son use his full potential in life. He might even be able to become a lawyer or a politician."

Sylvester had kept himself under control until now, but this was too much. "My son will NOT become a lawyer or politician," he said frostily. "And I'll thank you not to put such ideas into his head." He took a deep breath, adding, "If that was what you wanted, I think we can end the conversation right here. I've got some work to finish up outside."

Miss McKee must have seen the uselessness of continuing. She rose and picked up her flowered handbag. "I suspect you will be sorry for your decision," she said gravely, collecting her hat. "If you aren't, Andrew surely will be."

Sylvester got to his feet as well. "It's high time for him to stay home and learn to do a day's work," he said gruffly. "He doesn't need more books; he needs to learn to stick at some real work."

He stalked to the door and held it for her. "I'll bring your horse around."

Naomi had watched all of this without comment. She came around the table to shake the teacher's hand. "Thanks for all your work in teaching our children," she said. "We do appreciate it. They are getting a much better education than Sylvester or I did."

Miss McKee started to answer, but then changed her mind. "Bless you, Mrs. Martin," she said, and squeezed her hand. She followed Sylvester outside, and he gave her a hand up into her buggy.

That was the end of Andrew's schooling. Sylvester took him into his woodworking business as an apprentice. Andrew missed school, but like any normal thirteen-year-old boy, he was happy to lay aside the tedium of study to do a man's work.

Sylvester was a skilled instructor, and Andrew had already been helping in the shop for a few years, so the work wasn't new for him. But his father was also demanding, with a penchant for perfection that Andrew found difficult to satisfy.

One afternoon, Sylvester went to town and left Andrew to finish some work by himself. Naomi had been noticing the stressed look on Andrew's face the last few days and took this chance to talk to him about it. "So, how is it going in the shop?" she asked. "Are you enjoying the work?"

Andrew pulled a chair to the table and propped his head on his arms. "Oh, I don't know," he said morosely. "The work is okay, and I think I could enjoy it." He shrugged his shoulders. "But Dad is so particular, I can hardly do anything right for him."

He leaned back in his chair and Naomi saw the troubled look in his eyes. "He'll go over what I did this afternoon with a fine-tooth comb when he gets back. I know one thing already that won't be good enough for him. The chisel slipped a bit when I tried to put a slot in the side of a piece of wood."

Naomi looked at him sympathetically. "Is there anything you can do to fix it?" she asked. "I'll help you if I can."

Andrew smiled slightly at the idea of his mother doing precision woodwork. "We'd only make it worse," he said. "I think Dad will be able to fix it. I've seen him do the same thing and fix it. But I've never done this job before and I'm not sure what I did wrong." The boy's voice cracked in apprehension.

"Well, just take it patiently when he scolds you," Naomi encouraged him.

Sure enough, Sylvester asked Andrew at the breakfast table how the project had gone. "How did you get along notching that slot?" he asked.

"Um, I had a little trouble," Andrew admitted, clearing his throat nervously. "The chisel slipped some. It's not too bad, but I left it for you to look at. I wasn't sure how to get a smooth slot." He dropped his eyes to the mush he was eating.

Sylvester narrowed his eyes and opened his mouth, then he paused and glanced at Naomi. "Well, we can look at it when we get out there. You probably didn't check the grain of the wood."

Naomi watched them go out the door. *Why is it that sometimes Sylvester can take something like that without reacting and the next time it upsets him? Poor Andrew never knows for sure what is coming next. I hope he manages to hold himself together.*

Andrew became a good woodworker as time went on. In many ways, he was as skilled as his father. But Sylvester found it hard to let him work unsupervised, and Andrew still struggled with keeping his mind on what he was doing.

However, the thing that bothered Sylvester most was Andrew's tendency to forget to put tools away.

Naomi overheard one such confrontation when Andrew was about eighteen years old. Andrew had come in for lunch and was washing his hands when the door banged open and Sylvester came in. She saw right away that something had upset him.

"Andrew!" The young man jumped and dropped the towel. "Where did you put my hammer and awl? I've looked all over the shop for them."

Andrew turned to face his father and Naomi could see he was desperately trying to remember.

Then his face cleared. "I was using them in the driving shed yesterday to fix a harness," he said. "I might have left them over there. I'll run out and check."

Sylvester was washing his face and hands at the wash basin when Andrew returned. "Well?" he demanded.

"They were there," Andrew replied sheepishly. "I put them back on your tool board."

Sylvester grunted. Naomi wasn't sure if that was his way of saying thank you, or whether he was saying, *I told you so.*

"Next time put them away when you're finished," he snapped. "You waste way too much time trying to find things you forgot to put away."

It was a quiet meal.

Andrew can make me so mad. I don't know when he's going to learn to put his things away. Left my hammer and awl in the driving shed. I lit into him good about his carelessness. He'll never amount to anything if he doesn't learn to look after his things better. Good thing for him he remembered where he had left them and it didn't take him long to get them. I should have given him a good thrashing, even if he is eighteen.

It was customary in the Mennonite Church for young men and women to work for another family for a few years. Several farmers had asked for Andrew's help the year he was eighteen. But Sylvester had always refused. Andrew made more money for Sylvester by his free labor than he would have brought home by working away. But even Sylvester could bypass tradition for only so long. When a farmer came along the next February and asked for Andrew's help that year, Sylvester grudgingly agreed. He also let Martha go to work for another family as a hired girl. Suddenly, Sylvester and Naomi were home alone with only their youngest daughter.

"I'm going to have to hire someone to take Andrew's place in the shop," Sylvester grumbled to Naomi the week after Andrew left. "He did more work than I realized. There's no way I'll keep up without some help. Too bad Hettie isn't a boy."

So that was how twenty-year-old Edwin came to live with them. It took Naomi a bit to feel comfortable with having a stranger in the house, but Edwin was congenial and hardworking, and he even managed to get along with Sylvester most of the time.

Andrew came home for Sunday lunch several months after he had started his new job. He and Edwin sat in the parlor to visit. Sylvester went into the bedroom for a nap, and Naomi sat at the table to read her Bible. After a while, the conversation in the parlor attracted her attention.

Edwin asked, "So you prefer farming over woodworking?"

"Yes, I do," Andrew replied thoughtfully. "I didn't mind woodworking, but I really like working with animals and crops."

"My father wants me to be a farmer," said Edwin. "He's got a farm all picked out for me. All I need is a wife."

"Well, that shouldn't be a problem for you," Andrew laughed.

Edwin chuckled good-naturedly. "But I don't want to farm. I would rather have a shop like your father does, I suppose. But most of all, I'd like to go back to school."

"Really? What would you use your education for?"

"I'd like to be a teacher, or a writer." Edwin set his rocking chair in motion. "Someone who works with knowledge."

"It takes knowledge to be a good farmer," Andrew pointed out.

"Yes, but it takes interest, too. I dread the idea of farming for the next fifty years."

Andrew leaned forward and stirred up the dying fire. "Well, maybe you won't find a wife and then your farming problem would be solved. I suppose you could farm without a wife, but it would be a pretty lonely business."

"Sure would. Say, maybe we should have a double date some evening!"

In the next room, Naomi perked up her ears.

"Oh, I don't know," Andrew replied casually. "I'm not ready for that. If I could find someone like my mother, I might consider it, but I've never met any girls like her."

Naomi smiled.

"Your mom is a pretty good sport. I like her a lot."

"Well, she's learned about life the hard way," came the grim, low reply. "My pop is pretty hard to get along with sometimes."

Edwin's eyebrows lifted. "That's for sure. I noticed your mom toes the line pretty carefully. I had heard, before I came to work here, that your dad could be tough. It has actually gone better than I expected."

"What happens if you make a bad mistake, or forget to put a tool away?" Andrew asked curiously in hushed tones.

Edwin chuckled. "Oh, I've botched it a few times. But he gets over it. I just admit I made a mistake and carry on. I figure if I'm doing my best, I don't need to lie awake at night."

So that's how he gets along so well with Sylvester, Naomi thought. *And Sylvester seems to take to it.*

Andrew's discouraged tone carried clearly to the next room. "Somehow I've never found it that easy."

"Well, he's not my father. I'm here for a year and then I'll probably be on my way again, unless he asks me to stay on another year. It's different for you." Edwin handed Andrew a log for the fire. "It's too bad, though. My dad would rather have me farm, but I've got a good relationship with him and that helps a lot in working together."

Andrew arranged the log on the coals. "It sure does make a difference. That's how I am with my mom. I think I would leave home for good if it weren't for her," he admitted quietly.

Edwin glanced at his friend knowingly. "Well, *my* mom is a crab. She is always getting upset because someone tracked up the kitchen floor, or didn't do their work right. So, I guess I know a bit what it's like. But since I'm older, I'm not around her as much. I sure pity my dad sometimes. But he seems to love her anyway."

"Yeah, that's how it is with my mom. She won't talk back to my dad, even when he is really nasty to her or one of us children. Like I said, she has learned the hard way what happens."

Naomi wiped a tear from the corner of her eye. *So, he does see it,* she thought.

"Say, where does your dad go when he heads off for town?" Edwin asked abruptly. "No way does he have that many customers to look after. Sometimes he comes home whistling. Next time he is sour as a green apple. Something is going on somewhere."

Andrew shook his head, puzzled. "I don't know what he does. I think I'm better off not knowing. But every time he comes back he heads in here to his desk for an hour or two. Not sure why."

Edwin yawned. "Hey, let's go for a walk. Next thing you know, I'm going to fall asleep."

A Man and a Maid

17

There be three things which are too wonderful for me, yea, four which I know not: The way of an eagle in the air; the way of a serpent upon a rock; the way of a ship in the midst of the sea; and the way of a man with a maid.
—Agur, son of Jakeh

Edwin worked for Sylvester for three years. When he left, Sylvester asked Andrew to come home again to help in the shop. Good woodworkers were hard to come by, and Sylvester wasn't about to waste the training he had given his son. At first, Andrew was unhappy about this, but decided he could live with it for another year or two. Something else might come up after that. He was only twenty-two years old, so he had a lot of time.

Sylvester didn't say much, but Naomi could see he was pleased to have Andrew working for him again. Naomi, of course, was overjoyed. She had really missed Andrew during the three years he had worked away.

It was a good evening, the first time in over a year that the whole family was at home. Surprisingly, Sylvester seemed to feel something of the evening's joyful spirit. He even asked Martha about her work.

163

Martha was still working at the same place she had been for the last three years, and was going back to her job the next morning. Hettie was working away from home now as well, and she would leave soon for a new placement.

Sylvester started to fill in Andrew on the projects he had going in the shop. "We have a lot to do right now," he said, helping himself to the fried potatoes. "Joe Hiebert is building a new house for a customer and wants some cupboards and a few wardrobes. Things are booming in town, and I have had quite a bit of work recently."

Andrew was as surprised as Naomi was at these remarks, but he kept his reply calm. "Oh my, you must be missing Edwin."

Sylvester nodded. "He was a good worker. It surprised me how quickly he learned, for as little experience as he had. I'm really getting behind since he left."

The conversation became more general after this. Naomi asked Andrew how he had enjoyed his time farming.

"I really liked it," he replied. "I enjoy working with animals and crops. But I have been looking forward to being home again."

Naomi could tell he was being cautious about saying anything that might offend Sylvester, so she changed the subject. "It was strange not seeing you in church on Sunday mornings this past year, Andrew. Did you make some new friends at Morningdale?"

She noticed Martha and Hettie exchanging grins. "What do you girls know that I don't know?" she asked suspiciously. "Are you hiding something?"

Hettie shook her head mischievously. "Oh, no. We don't *know* anything." She emphasized the word in a way that told Naomi something was afoot somewhere. She made a mental note to corner Hettie and find out.

Andrew answered her question before anyone could carry on with the discussion. "I went to young people's singings and socials," he said. "I got to know all the young people there. Most of them were friendly."

"Were the girls friendly too?" Hettie asked, too innocently. "Or didn't you notice them?"

Andrew flushed. "Oh, they were okay," he replied lamely. Clearly, he didn't care for the direction the discussion had taken. "I didn't get to know most of them very well." He focused on cleaning his plate.

Sylvester had finished his meal and was listening to the conversation. He watched Andrew closely, a strange look on his face. Naomi noticed this. *It's almost as if he had never thought of Andrew being interested in girls. Surely he didn't expect him to stay home forever.*

Her attention shifted to Martha, who joined the conversation now. "Umm . . . what about Selina?" she wondered, eyeing her brother closely. "She worked at the same place you did, so you surely got to know her."

Andrew flushed again. "We went to young folks' gatherings and church together," he admitted. "I got to know her a lot better than the other girls. But she didn't have any other way to go," he added. "I wasn't going to make her sit at home when I was going away in an empty buggy."

The girls grinned at each other again, and Andrew snorted. "Now don't you get any big ideas, or count your chickens before they're hatched, you two. And you don't have to go around spreading any big stories."

The girls reacted to this scolding by exchanging grins once more.

Sylvester got to his feet, putting an end to the discussion. "Are you ready to go out to the shop?" he asked abruptly. "I need to fix a belt on the line drive, and I can show you what we are going to be doing tomorrow."

Andrew got up as well, glad to sidetrack his sisters. "Sure," he replied. "How's that new steam power unit working that you put in just before I left?" He followed Sylvester out the door.

"Pretty good," Sylvester replied. As they crossed the porch. Naomi heard him saying, "One of the best investments I've ever made."

Well, she thought. *Sylvester seems truly glad to have Andrew back again. I wonder if things will go better for them. It was good for Andrew to be gone for a while, if this is the result.* She turned to help the girls clear the table.

"So, what's this about Andrew and Selina?" she probed. "I hadn't heard anything about that."

Martha shrugged her shoulders. "We don't really know, I guess, but Cindy and her folks were up at Morningdale for church a while ago. She stayed for the singing, and she told us later how well Andrew got along with Selina. The young folks up there expect them to start dating eventually."

"What kind of girl is Selina?" Naturally, Naomi was curious. "Do you like her?"

Hettie answered first, as was normal. She was the youngest, but the more outgoing of the two girls. "Oh, she's fun," Hettie declared. "She would be good for Andrew. He's so quiet all the time and she would liven him up a bit."

Martha noticed the look on her mother's face. "Don't look so scared, Mom," she said. "Selina is a really nice girl. You would like her. She is naturally cheerful, and has a smile for everyone."

Naomi looked relieved. "Well, if she ever comes down here for church, make sure you point her out to me," she said. "That way it wouldn't be a total shock if Andrew decided to date her."

Hettie nodded. "We will. She is pretty, with wavy blond hair." She added, a little enviously, "I wish I had some of her good looks. Martha and I take after Dad in our looks, not you. I wish I could have seen you before you were married. You must have been pretty."

Naomi smiled. "Looks are only skin deep," she said gently. "I would be happy for Andrew to get a nice girl whether she was pretty or not."

Naomi thought a lot about her discussion with Hettie and Martha. She prayed about it, too. *I wish I knew that girl. And I wish Andrew would talk about it, if he is interested. I wonder how Sylvester would take it.*

The answer to Naomi's questions came sooner than she expected. Several weeks later Selina showed up in church, and Hettie came to Naomi after the service. "There she is," she whispered. "Over there, the girl with the blond hair." Wavy blond hair like Selina's was rare, and Naomi picked her out at once. True to Martha's earlier description, she was smiling and chatting with several girls standing with her.

"Don't stare, Mom," Hettie whispered. "She will see you."

Naomi pulled herself together and turned away, just as Selina turned toward them.

"Selina is going to be the hired girl for Angus Beachy," Hettie informed her. "So she is going to be staying around."

This gave Naomi something to consider, and she was quiet most of the way home. *Was this girl trying to 'catch' Andrew? Was she following him so he would ask her? I don't like girls who chase boys. That kind of marriage doesn't usually turn out very well.*

Andrew was quieter than normal that week. Things had been going well in the shop and Sylvester seemed to have accepted that Andrew could work without his constant supervision. Their working independently didn't take care of all the friction, but it helped. However, the week after Selina was at church, Andrew seemed to be in a world of his own, and Sylvester brought him back to earth with a jolt several times.

"Andrew!" The harsh bark was a little like old times and Andrew snapped to attention, dropping his fork in the process. "What is wrong with you the last few days?" Sylvester snapped. "I've asked you three times to pass the applesauce."

Andrew blushed, and Hettie giggled. "He is having sweet thoughts."

Sylvester's eyebrows drew together at this, and Hettie hushed. But it didn't keep her from winking at Andrew.

Her brother pretended not to hear her comment and changed the subject after passing the applesauce. "When are you leaving for your job?" he asked her. "It seems like you need something new to think about."

Hettie glanced at her father, who was busy eating applesauce and ignoring them both. "I'm moving out on Friday," she said. "So I have to tease you while I have the chance."

Andrew relented. "I will actually miss you," he said. "It won't seem right around here with you girls both gone."

Naomi agreed, though she didn't say anything. How would it be to live alone with Sylvester again, just as it was when they started out, if Andrew married?

Naomi never learned the exact details leading up to it, but several weeks after Hettie left for her new job, Andrew cleared his throat at the supper table.

"I'm taking Selina home after the singing on Sunday evening," he announced. "I might be home a bit later than usual."

Silence descended while Naomi and Andrew, hearts beating faster than usual, waited for Sylvester's reaction. His eyebrows drew together as he studied the lamp hanging over the middle of the table. "That wick needs trimming," he said gruffly to Naomi. "It's smoking a bit."

Then he added to Andrew, "Make sure you get home in time to do your work properly the next day." He pushed back his chair from the table. "I need to finish up some sanding in the shop, so I can stain that cupboard first thing in the morning. You finish the chores while I do that."

Andrew lingered at the table, finishing his tea and waiting to see what his mother would say. "I didn't know what Dad would think," he admitted, his tense shoulders relaxing. "At least he didn't get upset about it."

Naomi nodded. "I think he was expecting it. I know he was hoping for your help in the shop a while longer. He didn't get married until he was twenty-six, and he probably hoped you wouldn't either."

"I wouldn't have stayed home that long anyway," Andrew said decidedly. "I don't mind the work, but I'd rather be a farmer. I don't know if he will help me get started at that or not, but I don't intend to stay in the shop for more than a year or two. Dad is easier to get along with than he used to be, but you still never know how he is going to react."

Andrew seldom talked about his courtship except when he was alone with his mother. His father didn't mention the subject, unless Andrew was too sleepy on Monday mornings.

In fact, they ate their meals mostly in silence, except for remarks about trivial things like the weather or the garden. Sometimes Naomi's longing for meaningful conversation bubbled up like yeast inside her until she felt like screaming. But she doubted it would help much to do that, so she would ask Andrew a question instead, or talk about what she had been reading in her Bible.

Naomi still read her Bible regularly. It was the most stabilizing factor in her life. She noticed Sylvester always listened when she talked about what she had been reading. She had filled several notebooks with thoughts that were special to her. Recently someone had moved her notebook, and she suspected that Sylvester read it occasionally, though he never mentioned it.

"I was reading Matthew 18 the last few nights," Naomi remarked one evening, passing the potato soup to Andrew. "Jesus said in verse 3 that unless we are converted and become like children, we won't enter the kingdom of heaven. I wonder what He meant by that?" Sylvester didn't respond, but he looked a bit perturbed.

"My brother Adam talks a lot about being converted," Naomi added. "Only he says it means being born again."

Sylvester laughed disdainfully. "That's Methodist and Dunkard terminology. You are going to be led astray if you aren't careful."

Naomi looked puzzled. "But the Bible does say 'converted.' It also says, 'being born anew.' Nicodemus asked Jesus how this could happen. But you are right, most of our ministers don't use those words when they preach."

Andrew spoke up for the first time. "I remember Bishop George talking about that, a few months ago," he said. "It stuck with me because it sounded so strange. I had never heard anyone use those words before."

Sylvester's eyebrows drew together. "I say Bishop George had better watch himself. I know a lot of people who aren't happy with his preaching." He shifted in his chair. "I'm surprised he has lasted this long. He would be better off with the Dunkards."

Naomi and Andrew both liked Bishop George, but neither wanted to argue with Sylvester. Andrew changed the subject. "Would it be all right if I brought Selina here for lunch on Sunday?" he asked. "She knows Martha and Hettie from young folk's gatherings, but she doesn't know either of you very well."

Sylvester and Naomi looked at each other. They both knew this meant things were getting serious between the two young people. When Sylvester didn't answer, Naomi spoke: "I would love to get to know Selina better. She looks like such a nice girl. I've shaken her hand a few times, but we've never had a chance to talk."

Sylvester shifted in his chair. For some reason, he looked uncomfortable. He pulled out his handkerchief and wiped his forehead, even though it wasn't any warmer than usual in the room.

Naomi and Andrew waited for his response. "Well, I guess it's all right with me if it is with you," he finally said, looking at Naomi. "It's bound to happen eventually anyway." His grudging voice held something else she couldn't identify.

Andrew flinched, but he didn't respond. Instead he got up from the table. "I'll finish the chores before it gets dark," he said. "I can chop some more wood as well. Winter will be here before we know it." He headed out the door and Sylvester trailed after him.

Naomi watched them go. *Sylvester looks tired tonight,* she noticed. *I never thought of it before, but he is getting older. I hope he doesn't spoil the day for Andrew and Selina. They seem to be so happy together. I can't wait to get a chance to know her better.*

The local church district didn't have services that Sunday, so

Sylvester and Naomi stayed at home. Andrew, with a bounce in his step, went out the door to hitch his horse. *His buggy sure looks shiny this morning,* Naomi noticed. *He must have found time to wash it yesterday.*

Andrew's horse shared his master's exuberance, and he champed at the bit as Andrew drove out the lane. Sylvester had stepped out on the porch with Naomi to watch Andrew leave, his experienced eyes following the horse. Though he had given up horse training when his work in the shop became more demanding, he still liked a spirited horse. "That horse was a good buy," he commented. "He loves to run."

Naomi went back into the kitchen to put some finishing touches on their meal. Then she puttered around the house, straightening up things that weren't out of place and dusting spots that were already clean. Finally, she stopped herself. *This is silly,* she scolded herself. *This day will go fine, and Selina isn't coming to criticize my housekeeping. I'm becoming more and more like my mother.*

She stepped to the window and noticed that Sylvester had seated himself on the top porch step. *I wonder if he is nervous too? If it wasn't Sunday, he would be in his shop. That seems to be his refuge whenever pressure starts to build. He seems depressed this morning.*

She watched him for a few minutes. *I wish I could see inside his mind,* she thought for the thousandth time. *He wasn't this way when we started seeing each other. In fact, I was worried then that he was a little too flamboyant. He has really built a wall around himself. If only I could find a way through the wall.*

She stepped back from the window and went for her Bible as Sylvester came into the kitchen and crossed into the parlor. She watched wistfully as he shut the door behind him. *That's his other place of refuge. What does he do in there?* She shook her head and opened her Bible. *I guess this is my refuge. When life gets tough, he goes to the parlor and I go to my Bible.*

Meeting Selina

18

Rejoice with the wife of thy youth . . .
—Solomon

An hour later, Andrew returned and stopped at the front of the house to let Selina off. Sylvester must have heard them turning into the lane because he came out of the parlor and joined Naomi on the porch to meet Selina. To Naomi's relief, he was friendly as well as polite. *I wonder if Andrew warned Selina about him.*

Selina didn't seem nervous or uneasy at all. She bounced up the steps and shook hands with them. "I'm so glad to finally meet both of you." Her smile underscored her sincerity. "I've been looking forward to this all week."

She turned to Sylvester. "I've heard a lot about your cabinet-making skills. I'd love to see your shop. Would you give me a tour, even if it is Sunday?" Naomi could see that this request startled Sylvester, but he couldn't hide his pleasure.

"Oh, I think we could make that work," he said. "I'm doing some oak wardrobes right now. Oak is beautiful for making furniture. If it weren't so expensive, no one would use anything else."

Andrew rejoined them on the porch after unhitching his horse and giving him some water. Naomi led the way inside and took Selina's shawl and bonnet, placing them in the main bedroom.

After they had finished eating and clearing the table, Sylvester took everyone out for a tour of his shop. He seemed bashful as he opened the door, but Selina put him at ease right away.

"My, this shop is as clean as a kitchen!" she exclaimed. "I didn't know men could be this tidy." She turned to Sylvester. "Is it always this way, or did you do extra cleaning in case we came out here today?"

Sylvester smiled. "Oh, I try to clean up as I go, and I sweep up every evening. On Saturdays I do a little extra tidying up. It's always nice to come out to a clean shop on Monday mornings with everything in its place."

Andrew and Naomi glanced at each other. *This is a side of Sylvester we don't see very often*, Naomi thought. *I haven't been out here for months. I should show more interest in what he is doing.*

Andrew watched Selina's interest. "I guess that's one thing I didn't inherit from my father," he admitted ruefully. "I often don't remember to put my tools away, or clean up the shavings around my station."

Sylvester chuckled. "I'm still working on him," he told Selina. "By the time we pass him on to you, he might be fully trained." Everyone laughed, including Andrew, and Selina gave him a good-natured grin as they followed Sylvester down the aisle to look at the oak wardrobe.

Overall, it was a successful day. Andrew and Selina left after supper for the singing. Sylvester stayed in the kitchen for a change, rather than fleeing to the parlor. Naomi made a pot of tea, and they sat at the table relaxing while they discussed the day.

"What did you think of Selina?" Naomi asked.

Sylvester took a drink of tea, then set down his cup. "She reminds me a lot of what you were like at her age," he said. "I can't blame Andrew for going for her." He looked as if he wanted to add something else, but swallowed his words.

"She would make a nice daughter-in-law," he added after a moment of silence. He smiled. "I guess a woman would notice a clean shop. Good thing I cleaned up last night. I was so tired I almost left it. Never thought she would want to see it."

Naomi nodded. "She seemed genuinely interested," she said. "She's that kind of person, interested in other people and what they're doing." She flushed and fumbled with her teacup. "I was embarrassed to realize how little I get into your shop."

Sylvester looked at her, but she couldn't read the expression on his face. "You're welcome any time," he said. "I won't even make you sweep the floor."

Naomi blushed again. "You know, when we first got married, I was a bit upset when you asked me to sweep the floor in the shop."

He nodded. "I remember. Guess I didn't realize how you would take it." It was the closest he had come to an apology in a long time. "Hope Andrew gets off on a better foot than I did when he gets married."

The reminiscing seemed to make him withdraw. He got to his feet briskly. "I should check the animals before we go to bed."

Naomi stood at the window and watched him cross the lane to the barn. *So, he did notice. He must have felt badly about it but didn't know what to do. I wonder how many other times he has felt like that and I didn't realize it.* She stared blindly out the window. *Something, somehow, somewhere drove a wedge between us, and his personality hasn't allowed him to do anything about it. If only I could find out what it was.*

She shook her head and turned to clear the teacups and teapot from the table.

It was no surprise to Sylvester and Naomi when Andrew raised the subject of marriage one evening the following February. He cleared his throat, as he always did before broaching a difficult subject.

"Selina and I would like to get married this spring," he said, hands gripping his knees. "Her parents are willing. They have been expecting it and getting things together for her hope chest."

Naomi and Sylvester looked at each other. This time Sylvester responded first. "I have also been expecting it," he said reluctantly. "And I've been thinking. Jake Newcomer is interested in selling his farm, and it's a good place. Not so far away that you couldn't still help in the shop if you want to, or you could farm it yourself. I know your heart isn't in the woodworking."

This announcement was totally unexpected. Never, in his wildest dreams, had Andrew imagined this. Nor had Naomi. "Can . . . can we afford that?" she asked.

Sylvester looked offended. "Should be able to," he said shortly. "Unless Jake wants an outrageous price for it."

Andrew almost stuttered. "That would be . . ." he groped for the proper adjective, finally finishing with, "great. I never ever expected that."

"I'll talk to Jake this week," Sylvester said. "Maybe you could arrange with Selina to come along and look at it sometime soon."

"I'm sure she would like that," Andrew said. He could hardly stop smiling. "She was thinking we would need to rent for a while. The Newcomer place is a really good farm, from what I've heard, and the house and barn look nice too."

Andrew wants to get married this spring. I've had my eye on the Newcomer farm down the road. Good little farm for him, and the owner badly wants to sell. And Jim McCraw has a good team of horses that he broke in, the best team I've seen in a long time. Think I'll take Andrew to see them. About time to get him started in life. I wish sometimes that I wouldn't have been so hard on him while he was growing up. I figured it would do him good, and that he would forget the lickings I gave him.

But he sure is distant. Always quiet when I'm around,
like he is scared of me or something. Maybe it will help
if I give him a good farm.

One afternoon a week later, they all went over to see the farm. Jake was pleased to show it to them. "Always hoped one of the neighbors would want it," he said. "Don't like to see a lot of strange blood in the neighborhood."

Selina was ecstatic over the house. She and Naomi looked through it with Jake's wife while the men rambled around the yard and looked at the barn and outbuildings.

"The barn needs a bit of work," Jake told them. "A couple of beams should be replaced. I will help with that. I've always tried to keep everything ship-shape around here, and I want to make sure it is all in good condition for you."

There was too much snow on the ground to walk through the fields, but Sylvester was already acquainted with the farm and knew its reputation. "How many acres do you have?" he asked Jake.

"Sixty-five acres," Jake replied promptly. "About five acres in pasture, which you could break up if you want more cropland, and a couple acres in woodland."

Sylvester tugged at his beard before asking the fateful question. "So, what are you asking for it?"

Jake wrinkled his brow and eyed Sylvester. "Well, it's one of the best farms in the neighborhood, and prices have been going up over the last few years," he said. "How about $4,250?"[1]

Sylvester's face remained inscrutable. "Hmm. That's a lot of money. We'll have to talk about it." He turned to look at the house. "Let's see what the women-folk think of the house."

Jake grinned. "Yep, got to keep them happy, too. But we have kept

---

[1] This was an average price for an average farm, so it was a good price for a farm like this, which is probably why Sylvester didn't spend a lot of time trying to bring the price down.

the house in decent shape. The wife didn't approve of living in a shack while I spent money on the barn."

On the way home, Sylvester shocked them again. "I thought we would stop and look at a young team that Jim McCraw is selling. He broke them in himself and used them for a season."

He looked at Andrew. "You'll need a good team. Jim is one of the best horse trainers around. If he says this team is good, it's good. Especially if he's selling to a neighbor." Andrew already knew all this, but he was also aware that Jim McCraw had the most expensive horses in the county.

The afternoon had completely altered the perspective Andrew had of his father. He had never seen Sylvester spend this kind of money, even on himself, let alone one of his children. Sylvester usually bought things that would pay him back with big dividends. Andrew was too dazed to reply.

Jim McCraw was happy to show off his horses, even though he had never expected Sylvester to come looking for a team. He had done business with Sylvester before and knew how he felt about spending money. A big man with a booming voice, Jim grinned at Andrew. "So, you're looking for a good team of horses." His voice echoed through the barnyard. "Have we got some good news in the offing?" He looked at Naomi and Selina. "I see you blushing, young lady! But don't worry. I won't tell a soul."[2]

Jim hitched up the team, a beautiful picture of powerful horseflesh. He ran his hands over the flank of the closest horse. "See those muscles? These boys will go all day and ask for more. I used them myself last year, and there wasn't a team in the neighborhood that could keep up with them."

Sylvester already knew this, but he hadn't seen the horses up close before. He almost whistled as he examined them.

"Come on, Sylvester. You're a horseman. Tell me what you think

---

[2] Wedding plans were kept secret until the wedding was officially announced in church.

of them," Jim said. "Aren't they a set of beauties?"

"I'll tell you what I think after we've talked price," Sylvester countered. "You wouldn't take advantage of a poor man, would you?"

But his comments were halfhearted. These horses were worth a lot of money, and he knew it. And Jim was savvy enough to realize that.

Jim grinned again. "Poor man, indeed. I know from personal experience the kind of money you make on your cabinets and cupboards. Fortunately, I haven't needed one of your coffins." He chuckled at his own joke. "Here, let's hitch them to this wagon and take them for a trip around the barnyard."

There was no doubt. The team lived up to their reputation. High spirited yet steady, they stepped along like a dream come true. But Andrew could hardly believe that his father would spend the money for a team like this.

"Well, what do you think?" Jim said. "Solid oak with the best stain you can buy. It only *looks* like birch—the best oak always does." Jim smirked at Sylvester's pained look and his haunted glance at Naomi and Andrew. Jim gave the impression that he had been biding his time, waiting for an opportunity to fire some meaningful darts at the woodworker. An undercurrent ran between the two men that bewildered the others listening.

Naomi wondered at the sharp bantering. *Why would Jim be saying things like that? Sylvester doesn't sell birch cabinets and call them oak, does he?* Misgiving dampened the pleasure she had felt earlier.

Sylvester, who wasn't enjoying the show as much as Jim was, had evidently determined he would buy those horses. "What do want for them?" He cut Jim's chuckles short.

"Why, Sylvester," Jim answered, "these are the best horses I've ever raised. I should really be keeping them. But as a special favor," he emphasized, "you can have them for $125."

Sylvester's jaw dropped. An average draft horse was worth around $30.

Jim grinned. "That is for the pair, mind you. And a bargain they are. I wouldn't dream of insulting you by selling them to you for less than they're worth."

Sylvester was getting tired of the charade. "I'll give you $100 for them, if you throw in the harness," he snapped. "And not a penny more."

It was Jim's whose jaw dropped, though it seemed put on. "Sylvester," he said sadly. "I really don't want to be responsible for keeping you awake at night because I let you cheat me." Again, his tone held a meaning that escaped Naomi and Andrew, while Sylvester's face flushed angrily. "I can sell you the harnesses for an extra $10, if you want them. But I really couldn't take a penny less."

Andrew saw the chance of a lifetime slipping away, but Sylvester was made of sterner stuff. "You know as well as I do that you would never get $100 for them at an auction, with or without harnesses. I wouldn't offer you even that much if I didn't know they are the best workhorses I've ever seen."

Jim looked pleased. This, coming from Sylvester, was a compliment. But he was enough of a bargainer to take advantage of it as well. "See, you've told me yourself that they are worth more than an average team. Anyway, you can brag to your church people that you bought the most expensive team in the whole county for your boy."

Sylvester snorted. "And you'll brag to your drinking buddies that you talked old Sylvester Martin into giving you fifty dollars more for your team than they were worth."

The haggling continued for a while, since both men were master bargainers. This was a side of Sylvester that neither Naomi nor Andrew had ever seen, and Naomi hardly knew whether she should laugh or cry. But finally, Sylvester pulled $115 from his wallet, an exorbitant amount for a team of horses. For reasons known only to him, he handed it over to Jim. "We'll come over for them tomorrow," he said. "Mind you, don't swap those harnesses for an old set you've got lying around."

Jim grinned. "Nope," he said cheerfully. "If you buy oak you get oak, when you deal with me!" With this parting shot, he led the horses toward the barn.

The wedding took place several months later, in early spring. It brought back old memories for Naomi of the day she and Sylvester got married, memories she thought she had forgotten. Andrew and Selina were in their glory—neither could stop smiling. Bishop George conducted the ceremony and preached the sermon.

Naomi couldn't help contrasting Bishop George's sermon with the one her father-in-law had preached. *This is what a marriage sermon should be like. I wish Sylvester and I could have had this kind of start to our marriage.*

Sylvester sat rigidly beside her. As usual, Naomi wondered what he was thinking. *He has been so quiet. And he hasn't been behaving normally. He went all out in buying Andrew a good farm and the best team of horses he could find. And he paid cash! I had no idea we had that much money.*

She had even brought it up with him. "I didn't know we had that much money in the bank," she said timidly. "Andrew would have been happy with a lot less than what you have given him."

Sylvester hadn't given her a straight answer, just mumbled something about, "If we treat him right, he'll treat us right when we get old." That was all she could get out of him.

I wonder if he views this like an investment. But surely he knows that Andrew would have looked after us anyway. It's as if he is trying to make up for all the bad times he has given Andrew. I wish he would just come out and apologize, if that is how he feels.

Naomi brought her mind back to the wedding sermon as Bishop George gave Andrew and Selina some final advice. "There will be times in life when you wonder if your spouse still loves you," he said. "But don't let that drive a wedge between you. Lay your foundation in God and it will never crumble."

I have tried to do that, God, Naomi thought wistfully. *But it still hasn't worked. I know I have failed, and I have tried to make those times right. But somehow, I have never found a way inside Sylvester's heart or mind.* She wondered again what he was thinking. Was he paying attention to what was being said?

It seemed strange, coming home to an empty house after the wedding. The girls had returned to their jobs after the wedding. Andrew had moved his belongings over to his new farm the week before, but his wedding made his leaving more real. Naomi stirred up the fire in the stove, then started a pot of tea while she waited for Sylvester to put the horse in the barn. But her heart wasn't in what she was doing.

Now it really is just Sylvester and me again, she thought. The families the girls were working for lived too far away for them to come home much. Andrew was just a few miles down the road, but he wouldn't be back much either. He would be too busy getting his crops out this spring.

Sylvester came into the kitchen and pulled a chair up to the table as Naomi poured the tea. "Well, that takes care of that," he said. "I wish I could get Edwin back. It doesn't look like Andrew will be working much for me anymore."

Naomi sat down across the table from him. "How busy are you?" she asked. "Will you need to look for a hired man again?"

Sylvester shrugged. "Not sure," he said. "I'm not that keen on breaking in someone new. I already asked Edwin if he'd like to come back, but his father needs his help."

He stretched, then yawned. "I'm tired tonight, so maybe it looks bigger to me than it is. I'll probably try to work on my own again. Things have been slower the last while anyway."

A Time to Die 19

There is a time to be born and a time to die.
—Solomon

Life gradually settled into a new normal for Naomi and Sylvester. Naomi's highlights were the times she saw her children. Knowing this, her children tried either to visit her or meet her at church. Andrew seemed torn between wanting to see his mother and trying to avoid his father, but Selina took every opportunity to stop by and see Naomi. Invariably, she also took time to say hello to Sylvester. Naomi noticed that, in his own way, Sylvester looked forward to Selina's visits as much as she did.

It is interesting how Sylvester has taken to Selina, she thought after one of Selina's visits. *He always brightens up when she is around.*

In between Selina's visits, Sylvester tended to be morose. He got less work done than he used to, and several times a week he took time out to go to town. He spent most of his time either in his shop or in the parlor with the door shut.

He doesn't seem interested in anything lately, Naomi noticed. *He doesn't even seem to anticipate his trips to town. It's almost as if he feels he has to go.*

By now Naomi had some strong suspicions about why Sylvester was going to town so often. She kept telling herself that she wasn't sure. *I really don't know, so I shouldn't judge him. But even now it wouldn't be too late, if only he would trust me enough to tell me what is troubling him.*

Naomi often thought about how many areas of Sylvester's life she was excluded from. Yet a woman doesn't live with a man for twenty-five years without learning a few things about him, and it would have surprised him to know how well she understood him and his interests. She was keenly aware of the gulf widening between them, even though someone looking on wouldn't have noticed any change. As time went on, she felt a part of herself dying within her.

He's lost interest in me. If he ever loved me, he doesn't anymore. I wonder what, or who, has stolen him from me . . .

But those thoughts only led to discouragement, and she knew better than to dwell on them. She went back to her security—her Bible. Naomi's children offered some diversion from her pain, but it was her relationship with God that sustained her. And her Bible was how He spoke to her. She clung to God's promises as if He had spoken them just for her.

Naomi woke up one morning with a strange foreboding within, but she didn't know why.

At lunchtime, Sylvester came in as usual. "Guess I'll head to town this afternoon. Should be home for supper."

She leaned her chin on her hand and said wistfully, "Andrew and Selina haven't been over for a while. It's hard to believe they've been married for over five years."

He looked up and hesitated, then took another bite of bread. "I know. I could use his help this week, but he is busy with harvesting."

Naomi nodded. "I hope they are okay," she said, frowning slightly.

"I've had this strange feeling all morning that something bad is going to happen . . ." Her voice trailed off.

A startled look flashed across Sylvester's face. "I'm sure they are okay," he said. But he looked at her strangely before he went out the door.

Naomi watched him drive out the lane and down the road. Then she walked over to the cupboard and picked up her Bible, by now so familiar that she had little trouble finding what she was looking for. She sat down and read a favorite passage from Isaiah 43. *Fear not, for I have redeemed thee.* The words were a balm for her soul. *When thou passest through the waters, I will be with thee.*

She cradled her head in her arms and wept. And prayed. And wept some more. *God, you know where Sylvester is going. Please protect him. I'm afraid he's not ready to meet you. Please help him find you.*

Finally, she found a measure of peace. Walking over to the sink to wash her face in cold water, she heard someone drive in. *Is Sylvester back already?* She glanced at the clock and knew that he couldn't be. She went to the window and saw that Bishop George was tying his horse to the hitching post in front of the shop. *What does he want? Surely nothing has happened.*

Her heart fluttered as she hurried to the door and stepped onto the porch. Bishop George was walking toward the shop door, but catching sight of her, he came across to the house. "Is Sylvester home?" he asked pleasantly. "I was hoping to have a word with him."

Naomi shook her head. "No, he isn't," she replied. "He went to town this afternoon. He will be back for supper, as far as I know."

George scuffed at the ground with his boot, his brow wrinkled in thought. "All right. Well, when he gets home, tell him Preacher Daniel and I would like to talk to him this evening. We will be over after supper."

He glanced at some billowy clouds floating over the distant horizon, then turned back to her. "God bless you, sister," he said compassionately. Then he turned and walked back to his horse and buggy.

She watched him drive out the lane. *Why does he sound as if he feels sorry for me?*

It was suppertime and Sylvester still wasn't home. *I hope he gets here soon. The men could be here anytime. I really wonder what they want. Bishop George didn't look very happy. He seemed burdened about something.*

She wandered to the window, but there was no sign of Sylvester.

Half an hour passed, but he still wasn't home. She stirred the potato soup on the stove to keep it from burning, and went back to the window. Still nothing.

It was half an hour later when she finally heard a horse coming into the lane. She hurried to the window and sighed with relief. Another buggy was turning into the lane right behind Sylvester. *He just made it.*

She had no chance to warn Sylvester that he was getting company. He was startled as he realized the bishop and minister were driving into the lane behind him. He had almost finished unhitching his horse when the bishop pulled up to the hitching post. Sylvester said something to the men before he led his horse to the barn. Then the three of them walked to the house.

"I'm sorry you haven't had your supper yet," Bishop George was saying as they came into the kitchen. "We can wait while you eat."

Sylvester was plainly disturbed. He waved his hand irritably. "No, let's get it over with, whatever it is you're after. I can eat later." He didn't look at Naomi as he led the way to the parlor and shut the door tightly behind him.

But the closed door couldn't shut in everything that was happening. She heard the murmur of the bishop's voice, then Sylvester's petulant reply. Preacher Daniel said something, and Sylvester cut him off. Then the conversation became more heated, and she shuddered as Sylvester's voice grew louder.

The parlor was amazingly soundproof. But Naomi was also trying hard not to eavesdrop. In fact, sitting at the table, she covered her ears and tried to focus on other things. But she couldn't block out everything. "It's none of your business what I do!" she heard Sylvester shout.

Preacher Daniel tried to speak soothingly, but it didn't seem to be working. Then suddenly, in the middle of a sentence, Sylvester's voice trailed off, and she heard the bishop's startled exclamation. *What is going on?* she wondered. *Is something wrong?* She was just getting to her feet, alarmed by what she was hearing, when Bishop George pulled open the parlor door.

"Sister Naomi, come quickly," he called. "Sylvester has fainted, or taken a fit."

The rest of the evening blurred together. Preacher Daniel went for help, but it took over an hour for the doctor to arrive from town. By the time he got there, everyone knew he was too late to do anything but give the final verdict.

"Looks like an apoplexy," the doctor said gravely to Andrew, who had arrived with Selina just before the doctor showed up. "Must have been a serious one because it looks as if he was gone almost at once." He looked across the room at Naomi, who was crying in Selina's arms. "Make sure you don't leave your mother alone. I'll talk to your bishop about having the body cared for. I'm sure he will help you with funeral plans."

The next several days were a whirlwind of activity. Andrew built the coffin for his father, with the help of several of Naomi's brothers. As was customary, relatives, neighbors, and friends dropped in to view the body and give their condolences to Naomi throughout the next afternoon and evening.[1] Her brothers and their families surrounded her with support, as did Sylvester's relatives. Some of Sylvester's customers stopped by as well, though not as many as one might have expected. Jim McCraw, the horse trainer, came through

---

[1] Embalming was not common in North America until the twentieth century, and would have been unknown or frowned upon in Sylvester's setting.

and shook Naomi's hand, then Andrew's. "Never would-a thought it," he said, shaking his head. "Sylvester needed a coffin before I did." He wasn't joking, though Andrew knew he was referring to their conversation five years earlier in the barnyard.

The day of the funeral was hot and sweltering. Before the service started, they buried Sylvester beside his young son, the baby boy he had had such hopes for. It was a sober group who gathered in the local church house for the funeral service. Though few people knew the circumstances of his death, everyone knew Sylvester. Bishop George and Preacher Daniel knew what had happened, of course, but they kept their knowledge to themselves. George looked especially burdened during the service. Being a senior church leader, Daniel preached, trying his best to leave a positive note with his sermon.

I wish we had asked George to preach, Naomi thought during the service. *Somehow, he's more sympathetic. More real. Daniel means well but he seems to feel that he needs to preach Sylvester into heaven.*

Overall, it was not an easy day. After the funeral, the family and close relatives gathered at Naomi's house for a meal. Naomi went through the motions of eating and thanking people for coming, but afterward she remembered very little. Several days later, she had to ask Selina what had been served for the funeral meal.

Finally, everyone left except Martha and Hettie, who were staying with Naomi for the night. They tucked her into bed gently. "If you need anything, Mom, you just call," Hettie said. "I'll sleep on the daybed out here in the kitchen." She gave her mother a squeeze and slipped out, leaving the door ajar.

It took a long time for Naomi to go to sleep. Repeatedly she asked herself, *Did I do enough for Sylvester? Did I try hard enough to break down the barriers in our home? Why, oh why, wouldn't he tell me what he was struggling with?*

And the worst question of all, the question that had haunted her since he died so quickly: *Was he ready to die? Is there any hope at all for him? Where is he now?*

But the darkness had no answers. Finally, sheer exhaustion overcame her and she slept. Hettie peeked in at her in the early morning light and marveled at the peace on her face. "Let her sleep," she told Martha. "Her troubles will come flooding back to her soon enough when she wakes up."

It takes longer to bounce back from losing a spouse than most people realize. Sometimes Naomi felt that life was approaching a new normal for her, and she found herself laughing or smiling. Other times she felt a heavy burden akin to depression weighing her down. But no matter how her days went, she constantly felt a deep sense of loss, a feeling of guilt.

Why wasn't I able to meet Sylvester's needs? He seemed to love me when we got married, though he never told me so. But as life went on, he withdrew from me.

When the burden became too heavy, she went back to her old friend, the German Bible Sylvester had bought for her so many years ago. Somehow, the fact that he had bought it for her made it more precious. Sometimes she cried; other times she prayed. But always, she came away from her time with God feeling more secure, and most of all, loved.

God filled the gap in her life that Sylvester had never been able to fill.

She thought about that sometimes. *I wonder—if Sylvester had loved me like Andrew loves Selina, would I ever have grown to depend on God this much? But surely, every woman has a deep emotional need for her husband's love. Something deep inside her longs for his tenderness. That's not wrong, is it?*

Naomi broached the subject with Selina one day when they were together. Selina was the only woman with whom she felt comfortable discussing intimate subjects. Their mother-daughter relationship had grown into a deep friendship.

Even so, Naomi felt some trepidation as she spoke. She started in slowly. "I've got a strange question to ask you."

Selina looked up from the mending she was working on. "Sure, go ahead."

"Do you think a woman's need for her husband's love can be met by her relationship with God?" Naomi spoke hesitantly. "I'm not sure how to say this, but Sylvester mostly ignored me the last number of years. Earlier in our marriage we seemed to need each other, but that changed. I found myself depending increasingly on God to meet my longing for human love."

She wiped a tear from the corner of her eye. "Do you think I put up a barrier between us that Sylvester was afraid to cross?"

Selina put down her mending and gave Naomi her full attention. But it took her a few moments to formulate an answer. "I think every married woman needs her husband's love to feel like a complete person. Really, I think we need both the assurance of our husband's love, and the assurance of God's love."

She blushed a little. "I have never had reason to doubt my husband's love for me, or his need of me. But I feel that it has complemented my love for God, and my desire for the security of God's love. If I lost Andrew for some reason, I'm confident that my relationship with God would carry me through, but it would be a deep loss."

Naomi nodded. "But what if you felt you were at fault in losing your husband's love?"

Selina shook her head emphatically. "You mustn't blame yourself for the barrier between you and Father," she said. "If I know you at all, I'm sure you gave yourself to him unreservedly."

She got to her feet and walked over to the window, continuing thoughtfully. "It isn't normal for a man to back away like he did. For all his shortcomings, I'm sure he still had the human desire to love and be loved."

Still gazing out the window, Selina added softly, almost to herself, "I wonder where he went to release those desires, and why. There's a lot we don't know . . ."

Naomi bowed her head in agreement. "I've wondered that for a long time," she whispered brokenly. "And I might never know the answer. Sometimes I hope his journal will answer some of those questions. At other times,"—she paused to sip her tea—"at other times, I'm afraid it will."

Selina turned and gave Naomi an impulsive squeeze. "Please don't blame yourself. You are a wonderful mother-in-law and I'm sure you were a wonderful wife. But there are some things a woman can't do for her husband, and he has to find the way for himself. We can help and encourage, but if he refuses to accept our help, there is little we can do but pray."

Naomi wiped away another tear. "I did pray. I prayed every time he went to town. I prayed for him every time I opened my Bible. I still pray, even though I know it's too late."

She didn't say more, but deep inside, her thoughts continued. *Too late—what awful words! So final. Sylvester's times of decision are over, and there is no way for either of us to change what is past. I can't go back, nor can he. Wherever he is, I wonder if he is wishing as much as I do that we could go back and redo our life together.*

She didn't really expect an answer. But somehow, intuitively, she knew what the answer would have been, had she received one.

PART 3

Sylvester's Perspective

From Sylvester's Journal

  January 19, 1874: Amos Steiner was killed in a logging accident yesterday. He's younger than I am. Wonder if he was ready to die? Wonder if I am? Never really did talk to Naomi about that. She seems so at peace with God. I'm not. Death scares me. Surely people my age don't die. But Amos did. I hear that he was hard to get along with. Well, if God lets him in, I should be okay too. Hope so anyway. Though I'm not planning to die right away. Should have plenty of time to sort it out. But I wish I could talk to Naomi about it. If only I wouldn't be so stubborn.

Sylvester Martin

Too Late 20

Had I only lived my life for the Lord,
Had I only lived according to His Word.
Now my life is spent—it's too late to repent. Had I only . . .
—Alfreda Nightingale

Andrew closed the journal and pushed his chair back from the table. "Well, that's that," he said.

Selina looked up from her mending. "You're finished?" she asked.

"Yes, I am," he replied. "And I know my father a lot better than I ever expected to." He got to his feet and filled a tin mug with water at the pump by the kitchen sink. "Now I just have to decide what to do about it."

"Did you get any details about overcharging people?" Selina asked. "Did he talk about things like that?"

Andrew walked back to the table and picked up the journal again. He flipped some pages until he found a spot he had marked. "He talked about it. He seemed to think he had the right to make his own prices and that customers shouldn't gripe about it." He read one of the entries aloud.

April 19, 1843: *Got a good order today, from one of those Englishers who just moved into town. He doesn't seem to know the difference in price between oak and birch. I never told him what kind of wood I was quoting on. Just showed it to him and he went for it. I should make a real killing on this one. And then he wants me to build cabinets and counters for his new store he's setting up.*

Andrew dropped the journal on the table again. "That's from before he married Mom, so I guess it goes back to the very start of his business life." He added, "He doesn't give names anywhere, except he talks about the blacksmith toward the end."

He sat back down at the table. "You know, I've wondered a lot why he kept a journal. You hardly hear of men keeping journals. Well, at the very beginning, he explains why." Andrew picked up the journal and began reading.

March 18, 1841: *I turned 21 today, and Mother gave me a journal. She always kept one and she thought I should try it. Pop laughed at her and told her I would get over that idea within six months, and getting me a journal was just a waste of money. He's always making fun of us, and I'm going to prove him wrong this time. I'll write in this book until I die, or until I can't hold a pen anymore. Then we'll see who laughs.*

He placed the journal on the table. "Well, he certainly had a lot of determination. The book is almost full, and the last entry was the night before he died. I guess he was right about that part of it. It must have become a habit because he didn't stop even when his father died. Either that or he was just plain stubborn."

"It sounds like his relationship with his father wasn't very good either," Selina remarked.

"No, it wasn't," Andrew replied. "He doesn't even mention his father's death or funeral. He seemed to feel that his father was a hypocrite, even though he was a preacher." He flipped a few more pages in the journal. "Listen to this."

September 25, 1841: *Got together with some of the guys last night and had a few glasses of cider. Well, more than a few, really. Played cards and lost every game. I'm going to learn how to play like one of those gamblers someday. Good thing Pop was in bed when I got home, or he'd have lit into me. There's no question I've smelled liquor on his breath sometimes, but he sure gets uptight if he thinks I've been drinking. Don't know why. Most of the men in church take a drink occasionally. Including him.*

Selina shook her head. "Oh my, that's sad," she said. "It's no wonder he had some struggles."

Andrew pursed his lips. "It gets a lot worse than that. We'll have to visit Mother and go over this with her." He eyed her, his expression grim. "I'm warning you, it isn't pretty."

He took another drink of water, then set his cup on the table. Selina sat across from him and waited until he was ready to continue. He took a deep breath and let it out slowly. "I'm thinking maybe I should take this over to Bishop George and talk to him about it. I don't think my mother would mind, and I'd like advice on some of this. I've also got some questions he might be able to answer."

Selina nodded, but Andrew could see she was puzzling over something. "What are you thinking?" he asked curiously.

"Well," Selina replied slowly. "I'm just curious how *you* feel about your father now that you have read all of this." She waved her hand at the journal lying between them. "Did it make you feel worse, or better, about him?"

Andrew pondered the question. "I'm not sure, really," he said. "I don't feel bitter about him anymore. Like I said, I think I understand him a lot better than I did before I read the journal. Yet in some ways, I can't understand him at all. He kept talking about wanting to get right with God, but he claimed he didn't understand how." He reached for the journal again.

I asked Pop tonight how a person gets ready to die. I've never seen him so flabbergasted. You would think he never even thought about it. And he's supposed to be a preacher? He finally mumbled something about God deciding those things at judgment. But I don't know what good that would do me. It would be too late to change anything then, you would think.

"And this," he added, flipping a page. "This was a couple of weeks later."

Pop preached today. He said something about someone asking him recently how to get ready to die. I guess he's trying to figure it out too. His answer is to just do the best you can and God will sort out the rest. I guess we can't really know whether our best is good enough or not until we get to judgment. That doesn't sound like a very safe solution to me, but I'm sure I haven't got a better answer. Preacher George commented on Pop's sermon in his closing testimony. Said that if we truly want to find God, he thinks God will find us. But it seemed like he didn't dare say too much. The bishop was sitting right beside Preacher George and he started to look a bit like a thundercloud while George was speaking. When it was his turn, the bishop talked a bit about the Methodists and how they think they have all the answers and that we would do better just to let God sort things out than to become high-minded and try to take them into our own hands. Pop seemed to like that, but Preacher George didn't look very happy about it. I think I prefer Preacher George's approach. Might have to talk to him sometime. He seems like a nice person. He might have some answers for me.

"That must have been before George was ordained bishop," Selina commented. "It seems strange to call him Preacher George. But I understand what you're saying. Things have changed in church since your father was young. I don't think I remember a preacher ever talking like that."

Andrew raised his eyebrows dubiously. "I'm not so sure. I suspect that there are still quite a few people who would feel like that. Remember the message Preacher Daniel preached at Father's funeral? I don't think he would have a much better answer for how to prepare to die than my grandfather did."

His shoulders sagged. "I guess I do feel for my father a little. I've struggled enough in my own life, wondering who God is and how to get to know Him. It seems Father had a lot of the same questions. I just wish he would have talked about it."

"I'm sure your mother could have helped him," Selina said softly. "She's a real jewel of a Christian if there ever was one."

Andrew smiled. "Just like you helped me." He laid his hand on hers. "In some ways, you are a lot like my mother. But according to the stories she has been telling us, she didn't become that way overnight."

Selina blushed at the compliment, but focused on the second part of his comment. "None of us becomes that way overnight. I have a lot to learn. Your mother would say that she does too. Sometimes the tough seasons in life drive us to God."

"It was that way with my mother," Andrew agreed. "But I think she was always different from a lot of people in that regard. She refused to become bitter."

He reached out and picked up the journal one more time. "But she did struggle with those questions, it seems, and my father knew it." He flipped a few pages until he found what he was looking for. "This was after Mom's brother died. I didn't really know much about that before reading it in the journal. Listen to this."

Naomi's brother was killed in an accident this week. Sounds like he was drinking with some friends and fell out of the haymow. Naomi's pretty upset about it. He was pretty wild and she's afraid he wasn't ready to die. How does a person get ready to die anyway? I'm not sure I've ever heard a sermon about that. Maybe I should settle down a bit more, just in case.

"Here's the next entry," Andrew continued.

Naomi and I got to talking on Sunday night about dying. Odd subject for people our age, but it turns out she has the same questions I do. Her brother Reuben's death still really bothers her. He probably wasn't any worse than I am, but she is sure he wasn't ready to die.

Naomi and I decided to join the instruction class. She is still worried about being ready to die. For that matter, I am too, so maybe it would be good to get that taken care of. I still wonder if that is really all there is to it, but I guess it's a start anyway. At least Naomi seems to think so. I guess that will tie up my Sunday afternoons for the summer.

"Oh my," Selina exclaimed. "That is so sad. Did they really think joining the church would get them ready to die?"

"My father seems to have had his doubts too," Andrew said. "This is what he said a few months later."

We were baptized today. Can't say I feel any different than I did yesterday. Maybe that will come. Naomi was unusually quiet this evening. Wonder what she's thinking. Anyway, I hope God recognizes Mennonite baptisms. Not sure that I understand what they were trying to tell us in instruction class. I wish George could have had all the sessions. I think he understands God better than the other ministers do. For sure he knows Him better than the old bishop does.

Selina looked baffled. "Why didn't he just go and talk to George?" she wondered. "I'm sure George would have been able to help him. And he seemed to think pretty highly of George."

Andrew slowly closed the book, reluctantly meeting her eyes across the table. "It wasn't quite that simple," he said slowly. "I didn't read you everything he wrote." He paused. "He had some things in his life, even back then, that he knew he would need to confess." A heavy sigh escaped him.

Wonder what she would say about me, if she [Naomi] knew. Bothers me a bit. I'm sure she's a lot more faithful to me than I am to her. I almost came out and told her what I'm like, but something stopped me. I'm afraid she would never forgive me and then I'd lose her. And if the preachers found out, I'd be in real trouble. How does a fellow get out of a mess like I've made of my life? I must be going a bit daffy. Never used to think things like this. Oh well, Naomi might get it all figured out, then she can show me the way— if I'm not too proud to take it. Got to make some changes.

"I want to have my mother along when we go through those things. But that was a sample."

Andrew shook his head soberly. "He says that over and over again—'got to make some changes.' But he never did."

He closed the journal again, more emphatically this time. "He was still trying to find a way out on the last page of his journal."

Andrew went to see Bishop George the next day, dropping Selina off at his mother's home. He took the journal along and shared the same things with George that he had with Selina.

Bishop George listened quietly until Andrew finished, then he bowed his head. "If only I had known," he said softly. "I failed him. I knew for years that Sylvester had built a shell around himself. But it never dawned on me that he was struggling with unconfessed sin in his life and longing to find a way out of his trap."

He got to his feet and walked over to the small oil stove. Someone had lit it to take the chill out of the air in the parlor, which was normally unheated during the week. He turned it up a little, then held his hands over it, as if to warm them.

Andrew could see George wasn't paying attention to what he was doing. When he finally turned back toward him, Andrew was startled to see a few tears trickling down his cheek, losing themselves in his beard.

Bishop George sat down again before saying anything more. Even then, his voice choked up. "It has always been my worst nightmare—to have someone under my care be lost because I failed to realize the depth of his need."

"But it wasn't your fault," Andrew protested. "I'm sure you did everything you could, or that anyone could have done. Even my mother didn't know for sure, though I think she suspected it."

"I know," the bishop replied sadly. "But we can't bring him back. I'm sure God was merciful in giving him all the warnings and time he needed to find his way. But I just wish I would have talked to him."

Andrew hadn't thought of it from the bishop's perspective. And he was reasonably sure that some of the other church leaders wouldn't have worried much about it. He doubted that Daniel would, if he knew. But Bishop George, who always went beyond the call of duty, had a heart for his people.

"I guess I can see what you mean," Andrew said soberly. "My mother feels the same way. Yet I know she tried her best to help him. She spent hours praying for him. She told Selina she still prays for him, even though she knows it's too late to change anything."

"Your mother has a heart of gold," the bishop said. "I'm sure none of us realize how she struggled with this. I'm glad she has you and Selina to share her sorrows with."

Andrew nodded. "Selina has spent a lot of time with her," he said. "My mother seems to feel freer to share with her than she does with me or my sisters."

He paused, then changed the subject. "I've got a question, though," he said. "It seems my father really did want to find his way out of sin. Why didn't God make something happen to bring all of this out into the open, so it wouldn't remain a secret? It seems God would have been doing him a favor."

Bishop George pondered Andrew's question carefully. "I'm not sure," he said. "We can't read God's mind. But we can be sure God wanted your father to find his way. The Old Testament prophet Ezekiel says God takes no pleasure in the death of the wicked. But God does give us the freedom to choose our destiny. He never forces anyone to repent.

"It does seem your father wanted a way out," he continued gravely. "But apparently he wasn't willing to pay the price of true repentance. He wanted the reward without the cost. And that isn't how life works. Then suddenly, his chances were over.

"But I do feel," the bishop added, "that we haven't done enough teaching on this as a church. I know I haven't always talked about these things, mostly because I fear some people would accuse me of being a Methodist in sheep's clothing."

Andrew looked puzzled. "Why are our people against the Methodists so much?" he asked. "My uncle Adam is a very nice person, and he lives like a Christian should live. Yet he's Methodist, and it seems as if that is enough to guarantee that he will go to hell. At least in the mind of my father, it was."

George sat up straight in his chair. His face became so stern that it almost scared Andrew for a moment.

"No!" George was emphatic. "There is much more hope for a Methodist like your Uncle Adam than there is for a Mennonite like your father. I'm not encouraging you to become a Methodist. God knows we badly need spiritually-minded young men like yourself in our churches. But I absolutely refuse to condemn a person simply because he's a Methodist."

Andrew looked as surprised as he felt. "I just assumed all our church people felt like my father did," he said. "It was always hard for me to understand why anyone would feel that way about my Uncle Adam. We always enjoyed when they came over, though it always upset my father."

He eyed the bishop irresolutely, then voiced his question. "If you feel that way," he asked bravely, "why haven't you joined the Methodists yourself?"

George smiled, but looked weary. "I've struggled with the same question for years," he admitted. "But it just didn't seem like the right thing to do. God has called me to lead this part of His flock in the Mennonite Church, and as long as the Church will allow me to fulfill this call, I will stay. Also, even though I appreciate the Methodist and Dunkard teachings on piety and serving Christ, I still prefer the Mennonite practices in many ways."

Andrew knew enough about all three groups to understand what the bishop was referring to, without asking. Furthermore, it was high time for him to get home. He got to his feet, resting his hand on the chair back and turning to the bishop.

"I have one more question," he said slowly. "It may sound strange. But do you know anyone in town by the name of Susie Mae?"

A Trip to Town

21

Why wilt thou, my son, be ravished with a strange woman,
and embrace the bosom of a stranger? (Proverbs 5:20)

It was past chore time when Andrew left Bishop George's home, and he didn't have time to discuss anything with his mother when he picked up Selina. But they promised Naomi to get together the following Saturday afternoon to go over the journal with her.

"I'm sorry it has taken me this long," Andrew said to his mother while he helped Selina get into the buggy. "But I had to get myself into the right frame of mind to read it."

Naomi looked at him searchingly. "You seem to be more at rest than I've seen you for a long time," she said. "That means more to me than learning what you found in the journal."

She stepped back and watched them drive out the lane. "I do want to get this behind me as soon as possible," she told herself. "It won't change the facts, but maybe I can put it all to rest then."

Andrew was very quiet the rest of the evening. Selina learned why the next morning.

He pushed his empty plate back and refilled his tea. "I learned something from Bishop George that I would like to follow up on. I think I'll go to town this afternoon."

Selina looked up, startled. "What's up?" she asked.

"I want to talk to someone Father kept mentioning in his journal. I'd like to do it before we talk to my mother tomorrow," he replied. "It's pretty clear what was going on, but I'd like some verification if I'm not too late."

Selina was more disturbed than she let on. "Is it . . . is it safe?" she asked, remembering his trip to talk to Wes. "Is it that gambler again?"

"Well, I want to talk to him first, because one reason Father went to town that last day was to try to talk Wes out of collecting his gambling debts." He put down his empty teacup and got to his feet. "And Wes would probably know the other person I want to talk to."

Selina looked puzzled. "But who is that?" she asked.

Andrew stopped at the doorway to put on his jacket. There was a fresh nip in the air. Then he looked back at Selina. "Remember that box we found in his shop?" he asked tersely. "The one that came from SM?"

She nodded, and he took a deep breath. "SM stands for Susie Mae, and he went to town that day to say goodbye to her. She was moving away, so I might not find her. But I've got to try."

Selina's face blanched. "A woman?" she asked. Despite herself, her voice quivered.

Andrew nodded. "I'll tell you more when I get back. I wanted my mother to be the first to hear about it, but since I already talked to Bishop George about it, I might as well tell you, too. My mother won't mind."

He opened the door to step outside, then spoke back over his shoulder. "I'm not sure when I'll be back," he said. "Pray for me," he added. "This isn't going to be a very easy meeting, if I can find her."

Selina stood in the doorway and watched until he was out of sight. Then she sighed and shut the door. "Pray?" she said half aloud. "Yes, my husband, I'll pray. I won't stop until you're safely back."

Jim McCraw, the horse trainer, had retired and moved to town several years before Sylvester died. He was walking along the boardwalk with a friend, on his way to the saloon, when Andrew drove past him at a sharp trot. Jim stopped and watched the horse with admiration on his face.

"What a superb piece of horseflesh," he said. "That's one good thing Andrew inherited from his father—an eye for horses. He probably trained that one himself."

Then his eyes narrowed as Andrew pulled up in front of the saloon and jumped off his buggy, tying his horse to the hitching rail. "Well now, that's something I *didn't* think he inherited from his father," he said, surprise in his voice. "Never thought to see Andrew walk into a saloon."

His companion snickered. "He wouldn't be the first Mennonite to be a hypocrite," he drawled derisively.

"Not Andrew, though," Jim replied. "His wife and mother are two of the best Christians in the country, and he isn't far behind. Whatever he wants in that saloon, I'd wager my last dollar it isn't drinking or gambling."

"You're pretty sure of yourself." His companion eyed him dubiously. "I know a few things about his father."

"I do too," said Jim. "But Sylvester was Sylvester and his son is his son. They are as different from each other as father and son could ever be. Let's go in and see what is going on."

Andrew stopped inside the saloon doors to let his eyes adjust to the dim lighting. Even this early in the day, a few people sat at the bar and around the tables. He recognized the barkeeper from his last visit, and moved in his direction. Then he noticed Wes watching him from a corner. He stepped over that way, and hesitated.

The gambler responded to his unspoken question by nodding at a chair on the other side of the table. "Sit yourself," he said. "Haven't seen you for a while."

The two men measured each other across the table, but the gambler was the first to speak. "What's on your mind?" Then before Andrew could reply, he added, "How's your mother doing?"

Andrew answered the second question first. "She's doing all right, I think. Why are you asking?"

Wes took his time formulating his answer. "Don't know, really. I've just felt sorry for her since that day I went to see her. Can't see how a woman like her ever fit with a man like your father."

Andrew realized that if he was going to get any information from the man, he would have to be honest. "Well, life was difficult for her," he admitted. "Though you probably saw the worst side of my father. Still, it wasn't easy for her."

"It's bothered me a bit, the way I made her pay up your father's debts to me," the gambler said. "Been thinking maybe I should give some or all of it back. Don't feel right to rob a widow. Your father never had a chance in those card games. It was just like finding money on the street."

Andrew hadn't expected this kind of reaction from the gambler. He had been ready for anger or mockery, but not sympathy. He hardly knew how to respond.

Behind him the saloon doors opened again, and the gambler looked that way. "Huh," he smirked. "Looks like old Jim McCraw needs to wet his whistle."

Andrew glanced over his shoulder and nodded at his former neighbor. Jim and his friend moved on to a table just out of earshot, and ordered some coffee. This made the gambler remember his manners.

"Want a drink? Two cups of coffee," he called out to the waitress without waiting for a reply.

The waitress eyed him for a minute, plucked eyebrows lifted high, then evidently noticed the look in the gambler's eye and swallowed whatever smart remark she was about to make. Andrew waited until she brought the coffee before continuing the conversation.

"I think my mother would feel better if you kept that money," he responded to the gambler's earlier statement. "She feels bad about the hard deals my father apparently made here in town."

The gambler nodded, but commented, "Most of those guys had it coming, I always said. If they were stupid enough to let someone like Sylvester cheat them, they deserved to be cheated. I wouldn't worry about it myself." Wes dug a roll of bills out of his pocket, and peeled off a twenty-dollar bill.[1] "Here, give this to her, and give her my apologies for being so gruff with her."

He noticed Andrew's hesitation. "I'm not paying back what your father owed me," he said. "He deserved to lose that if he was stupid enough to imagine he could beat me at cards." He shook his head, "This is just a gift of sympathy, if she'll take it from an old sinner like me."

Andrew eyed the man carefully but he saw no sign of mockery on his face. "All right, I'll tell her that," he said. "And I'll go ahead and say thank you, for her."

The gambler ignored this and sat back, looking at Andrew searchingly. "But that wasn't why you came in here," he said, lowering his voice a little. "What's on your mind?"

Andrew took a deep breath, steadying trembling hands on the scarred table. "Who is Susie Mae?" he asked. "And is she still in town?"

---

[1] Between $400 and $500, in today's money.

Jim McCraw and his friend sat there quietly drinking their coffee. But neither of them paid a lot of attention to the taste (it was just saloon coffee, after all). They were watching the interchange between the gambler and Andrew. They had purposely chosen a table out of earshot, in order not to eavesdrop on the conversation. But both could tell it was serious, and they noticed the gambler give some money to Andrew. They also noticed Andrew's hesitation in taking it.

"Something funny going on over there," grunted Jim.

"For sure," agreed his friend. "Never saw Wes give someone cash like that without him being forced to. And they haven't even been playing."

Jim was watching closely when Andrew asked his last questions, and he saw Wes's startled reaction and the way his eyes narrowed. He saw him lean forward and speak in a guarded tone, and saw Andrew's response.

Then Wes got to his feet and shoved a weather-beaten cowboy hat onto his head. Andrew followed him, walking past Jim without making eye contact. But Jim heard the gambler's words: "I'll take you over there. They wouldn't let you in if you came by yourself."

Jim and his friend exchanged a glance, then got to their feet in unison. "Told you something funny was going on," Jim said grimly.

They walked to the door and stood in the shadows, watching Andrew and the gambler walk up the street and cross the road to an old house. Wes opened the door and stepped inside with Andrew at his heels. Jim took a deep breath. "Well I'll be . . ." He left the rest of the phrase unsaid, but any onlooker could have seen he was shocked.

His friend seemed to share his surprise. "You sure your friend Andrew isn't a hypocrite?" he asked skeptically. "There's only one kind of person goes through the doors of that house. I've seen Sylvester go in there a time or two, but if Andrew is what you say he is, he sure doesn't belong in there."

They turned and went back into the saloon.

It was close to an hour and several mugs of coffee later when Wes returned. He slouched across the stained wooden floor to his spot in the corner and ordered a drink. It wasn't coffee this time, Jim noticed, but something stronger. Outside the window, he saw Andrew's horse and buggy leave.

He shrugged his shoulders and said to his friend, "I suppose we'll never know, because I'm sure not going to ask Wes what that was all about."

His friend took another swallow of lukewarm coffee and made a face. "This coffee gets worse every time we come in here," he said. "So are you still sticking to your defense of Andrew Martin? Or is he a hypocrite like his old man was?"

Jim drained his coffee cup and pulled out his wallet to pay the bill. "Nope, I'm holding tough on that one," he asserted. He dropped the money on the table and both men got to their feet.

From his corner, Wes watched them go, then ordered another drink.

It was a long trip home for Andrew. On one hand his trip to town had been as successful as he could have hoped. On the other hand he had learned some things he really didn't want to know. But somehow what kept tugging at him the most was the strange reaction of the gambler, Wes.

It's odd, the way he has taken pity on my mother, he thought. He shook the reins, urging his horse to more speed.

His mind went back to Wes. *I can hardly believe he gave me twenty dollars to give Mother. And he apologized for asking her for money in the first place. That will shock her, for sure. He frightened her when he came to the house. It seems that a godly response can touch the hardest heart.*

He thought longingly of Selina at home praying for him. He shook the reins again. *Can't wait to see her. I wonder if my father ever felt this way about my mother. I think he did, but maybe he didn't know how to tell*

tell her. *His one big failure must have always stood between them, even if she didn't know about it.*

He took a deep breath of chilly air, savoring it as long as he could. It was good to have this trip behind him. Now he needed to visit his mother and then they all could put that whole episode behind them.

I never ever realized the problems that one person's sin can make for other people. Surely, Father would have done something about it if he had realized how the rest of us would feel. At the very least it seems he would have burned that journal. I guess he just didn't expect to die that quickly.

He thought back to his talk with Bishop George and remembered the tears running down the bishop's cheek. *It isn't just the family members who have been affected. If I know Bishop George at all, this will haunt him for a long time. I suppose none of us will ever forget this.*

The steady clip-clopping of the horse's hooves and the whirring of buggy wheels were soothing to Andrew, and the entire day seemed brighter as he neared home.

Home. And Selina.

He thought again of her promise to pray for him. And for the hundredth time he prayed, *God, I pray I won't let her down, like my father let my mother down. Help me to be worthy of her and love her as she deserves.*

Selina was watching at the window when he drove in. He waved to her and headed straight to the barn with his horse. *I'll start the chores while she gets supper on,* he thought. *We'll have a lot to talk about tonight, I suspect. I had better tell her the whole story as I know it. Some of the details we'll never know for sure.*

Chores didn't take as long as he expected because Selina had been in the barn and done a lot of them. He finished up the feeding and milked the few cows they had, then strained the milk. He would take that to the ice house to cool, and later scoop the cream from the top.

He made his way to the house through the deepening twilight.

The yellow lamplight in the kitchen windows beckoned him, and the cheerful light warmed his heart as he opened the door. Selina met him with a quick hug before she put the last touches on the supper table.

It was a cheerful and relaxing meal. Andrew told her about meeting with the gambler, and his conversation with him. Selina gasped when he pulled the twenty dollars out of his pocket.

"You mean he wants to give that to your mother?" she asked. "Whatever made him do that?"

"I don't know," Andrew replied. "I have been thinking about that all the way home. It is almost as if he had never met a Christian woman before."

Selina tilted her head as she considered this. "Or he might have had a Christian mother, and your mother reminded him of her. Maybe he was taught well but then turned his back on God later in life."

"Maybe," Andrew said. "I don't think I'd want to ask him, though. He was pretty soft today, for some reason. But I suspect he could be pretty tough depending on the situation. I'd hate to push him the wrong way."

Selina nodded. "Wouldn't it be wonderful if we could help someone like that?" she asked wistfully. "You know, I don't think I've ever met someone who became a Christian and joined our church. The Methodists sometimes help people like that. Why can't we?"

Andrew's eyes widened as he stared at her. "That would be a first, all right. I can't imagine how people's jaws would drop if we brought Wes along to church."

"But why?" Selina persisted. "Isn't that why we're here?"

It was a new thought for Andrew, but the more they talked about it, the more he agreed with Selina. "I can see what you're saying," he said thoughtfully. "We've fallen a long way from what the Bible teaches in some of these things."

He started to clear off the dirty dishes and take them to the sink. "I'll have to talk to Bishop George about that sometime."

It wasn't until they finished the supper dishes and were relaxing that Selina raised the question lurking in her mind all evening.

"Did you find Susie Mae?"

Andrew laid down the newspaper he had bought in town and sighed heavily.

"Yes, I did. Wes knew where she was and took me over."

Who Is Susie Mae?

22

Why did you steal my husband?
—Naomi Martin

Saturday afternoon hardly came soon enough for Naomi, but it came too soon for Andrew. However, like Naomi, he wanted to get the journal behind him and done with. It had hung over his head like a dark cloud for months, and it was time to move on.

"I'm glad Bishop George and his wife are coming over this afternoon, too," Andrew told Selina as they drove out the lane. "I think this is going to be a hard meeting."

"Do you think your sisters will be there?" Selina asked. "They know about it, don't they?"

Andrew shook the reins, and his horse lengthened its stride. "I'm not sure," he replied. "I think Mother invited them, but I don't know what they decided. Martha hates controversy of any sort, and Hettie is still pretty upset at Father."

"I can't really blame them for not wanting to be there," Selina said thoughtfully. "I can't imagine what it must be like to discover something like this about your father." She pulled the heavy lap robe a little tighter around her legs to keep out the wind. She shivered a little. "My, I'm not used to this chilly weather yet. It looks like it might snow today."

Andrew hadn't noticed the weather. "I guess you're right," he replied. "But if we can get this afternoon behind us, it can storm until spring for all I care."

Selina smiled. "You might change your mind about that after a week or two," she suggested. Then she sobered, "How are you going to do this? Are you going to read the whole journal?"

Andrew chewed his lip. "I'm not sure. I don't really have the heart to read everything to my mother. But we'll have to go over the basic facts, and see if she has any questions."

They turned into Naomi's lane and noticed that Bishop George and his wife were already there. "It doesn't look like your sisters are here," Selina commented. "Maybe you'll have to talk with them later."

George and his wife, Nancy, were already seated at the table drinking tea when Andrew and Selina entered the kitchen. George looked up with a smile. "Chilly out there," he remarked to them as they took off their coats. "But I guess it will get worse before it gets better."

Andrew and Selina smiled back at the older man. "It's good to get out of the house and get some of the cobwebs out of my lungs," Selina said. "I like brisk weather."

Nancy shivered at the thought and took another sip of her tea. She was a kind grandmotherly woman, an excellent partner for Bishop George. "I'm already looking forward to spring," she said. "But in the meantime, this tea really warms me up."

Naomi smiled and refilled Nancy's cup, pouring some for Andrew and Selina as well. "I'm sorry I can't offer you coffee," she said. "Sylvester didn't like coffee, and we never had it in the house."

Andrew sat down and took a drink. "This is better than the coffee I had at the saloon yesterday," he said. "They use only half enough coffee beans. Tastes like dishwater." He made a face, then added, "Not that I've ever tried drinking dishwater."

Bishop George eyed him from his chair at the head of the table. "Well, the coffee they serve at that saloon is still better than almost everything else they serve there," he said pointedly. "I'm glad you were drinking coffee rather than hard cider or whiskey."

"The only reason I went in there was to talk to the gambler, Wes." Andrew smiled, then added, "Wes ordered the coffee. I wonder when the last time was that he drank coffee there. I don't think it is his normal drink."

Bishop George nodded. "Did you get your questions answered?" he asked. "Was he cooperative?"

"Yes," said Andrew. "It was strange, almost." He dug into his pocket and pulled out the money Wes had given him and handed it across the table to his mother. "He sent this for you, and apologized for being so gruff when he was here."

Naomi eyed the money a bit distastefully. "Sylvester owed it to him," she said. "I don't really want it back."

"I told him that," Andrew said. "But he said this isn't paying back what Father owed but a gift from him, for whatever reason. He said Father deserved to lose what he lost. He doesn't have a very high opinion of Father. But he does of you, and he said he shouldn't have made your load heavier."

Andrew pulled his chair closer to the table. "I think you should take it. He's not the kind to pay out that kind of money lightly."

He opened the journal and turned back to the bishop. "Why don't you take charge. I'll tell you more about my meeting with Wes when we get to that part of the story."

Bishop George nodded. "Let's pray first," he suggested. "This isn't going to be an easy meeting for your mother or you."

Andrew agonized over how to tell his mother what she needed to know, without hurting her unduly. He ended up going over the same parts of the journal he had presented earlier to Selina and George, leaving the most devastating parts unread for the moment. "I do feel a little more sympathy for my father since I read this," he said when he finished. He looked at his mother. "He did realize what he was putting you through, and he felt bad about it sometimes. Let me read you part of one entry he made this summer."

Came home and Naomi was so happy to see me. She had a delicious supper ready. I just about couldn't eat it, I felt so guilty about the way I treated her.

"That was the week he died," he added.

Naomi looked disturbed. "But why couldn't he tell me that?" She shook her head. "Even just that much would have gone a long way in healing our relationship."

Andrew looked at his mother compassionately. "Because he felt guilty and unworthy of you," he replied. "He was struggling with that guilt even before you were married. Remember one of the early journal entries, during your courtship, when you had been talking about Uncle Reuben's death? He wrote that he wasn't sure he was ready to die, and he was afraid if you found out some of the things he had done, you would never forgive him and he would lose you."

The room was quiet for a few moments. Then Naomi whispered, "I remember that night."

She lifted her hands, bewildered, and said in frustration, "But what was he guilty of? At that point, we had been courting for only a short time. We barely knew each other."

Andrew took a deep breath and looked at Selina. She gave him an encouraging smile from across the table. "He had his eye on you from the time you moved into the area," he began, handling the painful area as gently as possible. "He was pretty impressed. But before he asked you out, he got himself into some kind of trouble. Let me read you some more."

He fumbled the pages backward until he found what he was after.

Snuck out to town last night and sparked old man Turret's daughter for a while. She's as "English" as they come, but she doesn't care if I'm a Mennonite or a Frenchman. I need to get myself a good wife. I'm tired of doing my own cooking and washing, like an old maid. I would never marry someone like old man Turret's daughter, but she was sure fun.

He jumped on to another entry before his mother had time to react. "This one was three days later," he said grimly.

Well, I bit the bullet and took Naomi home from the singing last night. She's a bit too religious for my taste. I get enough of that every month when we have church. But she was fine when I got her a bit distracted. I guess she thought that with me being a preacher's son and all that, she needed to show how pious she could be. Things are looking up, Sylvester my boy!

His mother looked shocked. "He was doing this when he asked me to court?" It wasn't really a question. "How could he do something like that to me?"

Everyone at the table could see how the news jolted her. "I had no idea." She shook her head, pain etching her face. "Did nobody know? Why didn't somebody warn me?"

She paused, then thought of something else. "What does he mean by 'sparking her'? How far did this go?" She tried to firm up her trembling voice.

Andrew shrugged. "He doesn't say. But it was enough that he felt he couldn't tell anyone without serious repercussions." He glanced at the journal again. "Here is an entry several months later. Apparently, he had bought a horse to break in."

Took a chance today. I picked up Susie Mae (old man Turrett's daughter) at the store where she works and took her for the ride of her life with my new horse. Scared the wits out of her! Almost got caught though. Preacher George came around the corner in town just as we went by. Fortunately, he didn't notice me. I'll have to be more careful. If word got back to Naomi, she might not like it so well. I should really stop going to see Susie Mae, I guess. She knows that I'm going to marry Naomi some-day. Doesn't seem to care. She just wants some excite-ment. Kind of like me, I guess.

Naomi opened her mouth, then closed it without saying anything. Breathing heavily, she tried again, saying haltingly, "Susie Mae. That was . . . the girl who worked . . . at the general store. She . . . she might still work there, for all I know." She blew her nose. "I'm sorry for being so weepy," she said. "But this is . . . such a shock. I met her a few times. She was always friendly, and asking about the chil-dren . . ." Her voice trailed off.

Then she looked up again. "Susie Mae. SM. That box we found in the shop after Sylvester died was from someone with those ini-tials. It was from her, then." Naomi's voice was leaden, like some-one who was forcing each syllable through a heavy blanket of fatigue.

Andrew nodded, rising. "I want to check his desk again. He said in the journal that the gift was a miniature from her. He didn't have a chance to hide it properly, so it might be in there."

No one spoke while he was in the parlor. In a few minutes he was back, carrying a small frame with a picture in it. "I'm not sure why I missed it the other time," he said. "I guess I was looking for something larger and didn't notice it."

He handed it to his mother, who gazed at it for a long time. "Yes, I've seen her," she whispered. "And she . . . she is the woman who took my husband from me." She buried her head in her arms. "God have mercy on her, and Sylvester," she cried out brokenly. "I wonder if she realizes what she did to me."

Andrew's lips tightened. "Oh yes, she does," he replied grimly. "You see, I talked with her yesterday."

All eyes focused on him. Selina was the only one there who had heard this news. "Yes, she realizes," he repeated. "I hope I wasn't too hard on her. Wes, the gambler, was standing there and heard the whole exchange, so I tried to be careful. In fact, when we got back out on the street, he told me I was too easy on her. 'Your mother is a good woman, and she didn't deserve what Susie Mae did to her,' he said."

Andrew paused. "Well, he actually used some words I don't want to repeat. He was pretty stirred up. In fact, he shook his finger in my face and told me, 'If your wife is like your mother, then whatever you do, don't treat *her* like your father treated your mother. Women like that are worth their weight in gold.' Then he shut up and headed back to the saloon."

He took another deep breath. "I think she knows what she did to you." He looked at Naomi, "She was crying when I left. I don't know whose fault it was, really, Susie Mae's or Father's. I think they were both just too morally weak to do what they knew was right."

Selina quietly got to her feet and poured more tea for everyone while this information soaked in.

Finally, Andrew broke the silence. "I guess I feel a little sorry for Susie Mae. She has ruined her life and has no real chance of happiness. Father knew that too. Here's an entry from around the time Martha was born."

Met Susie Mae today. She stopped and talked again. Seemed glad to see me. More like I was an old friend than an old flame. Maybe I've been too tough on her. She gets lonely sometimes. Most of her old boyfriends have gone on and married other girls. She's growing older too, but no one wants to be around her because of her bad reputation.

"There was a time during the early years of your marriage when he completely avoided Susie Mae," he told Naomi. He turned back to some more entries in the journal. "He wrote this the night before you got married."

The next time I write in this journal I'll be a married man. Feels strange in a way. Am I giving up my freedom, or gaining a relationship? Maybe both, but I'm going to give it a good try. Naomi's too nice a girl to let down. I went out to see Susie Mae today for the last time. I told her this was goodbye, that I wouldn't be taking her out anymore, and that I was turning over a new leaf. I meant it too, but she just laughed and said, "We'll see how long it lasts this time." Sort of irritated me, but I guess she is right. I broke up with her about three times before this and ended up going back when I got lonely. Should have no reason to get lonely now anymore. Still haven't figured out my question about being ready to die, though. Maybe Naomi and I can sort it out together. Hope so. I'm not sure why this thing haunts me like it does. It is almost like a premonition that I'll die unexpectedly and won't have a chance to sort it out.

Everyone looked startled as Andrew read the last several sentences.

"He was right," Bishop George said soberly. "God warned him, years before it happened."

Andrew nodded. "Yes, I think he knew what he needed to do. He keeps talking about Susie Mae occasionally—how he saw her but ignored her, how she winked at him, how she met him in the baking aisle and snickered. It troubled him." He flipped a page or two again. "Like this . . ."

Saw Susie Mae in town again. She was stocking shelves at the store. I decided to keep on ignoring her. It is safer that way. I wish there were another store in town, so I could avoid her totally. She is part of the past for me and that is where she is staying. I wonder if I should tell Naomi about her. But I'm afraid she would never respect me again. I can't figure out why I ever let myself into a trap like that. What would people think if they found out? Wish I could forget the times I spent with her.

Bishop George shook his head sorrowfully. "Be sure your sin will find you out," the Bible says. "The way of the transgressor is hard."

"He resisted her for about ten years," Andrew said softly, knowing his words brought further pain to his mother. "But things started to go harder at home. The two of you disagreed over child training and a few other things. It sounds like he caved in one time when he went to town while he was upset with you," he told his mother.

I should learn not to go to town when I'm upset with Naomi. I met Susie Mae in town and spilled out to her. Not a good idea, because she gave me a hug and tried to console me. Said that anytime I needed a warm shoulder to cry on, I could come to her. Can't understand the power that woman has over me. Wish I would never have set eyes on her.

"He didn't say much about her for a while, but about five years later, he wrote this," Andrew continued.

> *Told Naomi I was going to town to see a customer today. Stopped to visit with Susie Mae and she gave me a bite to eat. I told Naomi I ate in town. She has learned not to ask questions about things that don't concern her.*

"And three years later . . ."

> *Been seeing more of Susie Mae. I get a bit tired of family life. Naomi is a good worker, but she has lost most of the spice she had before we were married. Maybe she would say it is my fault, but my pop always said that a man needs to teach a woman where her place is. Of course, he never said anything about what that did to the woman. But my mom used to just spit right back at him when he got under her hide.*

"You can see how he went downhill after he let go," Bishop George observed sadly. "If only he could have held on, and found his way with God. But it seems like he never was able to be strong enough."

"He knew that Mother had found what he himself so badly wanted," Andrew said. "Here are a couple more entries."

> *Got Naomi some notebooks and a few pencils today. She wants to take notes while she is reading her Bible. She doesn't think anyone will read them, but I wouldn't mind seeing what she is thinking. She has really come back to life since she started reading that Bible. I think it was a good investment anyway.*

"This one was six months later."

Naomi and the children went over to her parents today for a while. I went into the house after she left and found her notebooks and read some of them. I was surprised. She would have made a good preacher if she had been a man. I had no idea how serious she takes this thing of living for God. Almost makes me jealous.

Naomi had cried herself out and was listening quietly to all this. "I had no idea," she said softly. "There is so much about my husband that I didn't know. If only I had been a better wife for him."

Selina gave her a squeeze, and Nancy hugged her from the other side. "You did very well for your situation," Nancy told Naomi. "Please don't blame yourself."

Bishop George nodded his agreement. "Yes, sister, that's right. Of course, you made some mistakes. We all do. But you did everything humanly possible to rescue Sylvester."

Andrew sighed. "I should just let you read the whole book for yourself," he offered. "I'm not reading nearly everything. He said a lot of good about you, and a lot of bad about me. He never said much about the girls, but he was really bothered about me."

He looked across the table at Selina. "But he changed his tune when Selina came along. He seemed to like her. It reminded him of his courtship days. Then he started looking for ways to get me to like him. Here's what he wrote the night I brought Selina home the first time."

Andrew brought Selina home today. Things look pretty serious for them. Next he will want to get married. I guess he is old enough. Several of his friends are married already. She is a nice girl, a lot like Naomi was before we got married. I wonder why Naomi has changed so much. Really makes me wonder if I have been too hard on her. I hope Andrew doesn't do that to Selina. I'm afraid it is too late for Naomi and me. And Susie Mae is always hanging over me. I guess that is as much my fault as hers. Wish I had never gone into that store that first time. But I can't confess now. Everyone would be horrified. Somehow this evening brought back so many old memories of when Naomi and I first kept company. If only I could go back there and start over.

Again, Naomi listened carefully. "Oh, Sylvester," she said brokenly. "If only we could both go back there and start over. You have no idea how much I wish we could have a second chance."

She sat quietly for a moment, steeling herself for her most difficult question. "Just one more thing, and then I'm satisfied." She steadied her voice. "Did they ever sleep together?"

Again, every eye was riveted on Andrew, who answered slowly. "It appears they did," he said reluctantly. "He alludes to it twice in the journal, both times after you and he were alone again after we children had left home. The first time he says he fell again, so I don't know when it started. Maybe the other time was way back before you were married."

Naomi bowed her head for a moment. When she looked up, her eyes flashed like old times. "Take that book away," she said fiercely, waving her hand at the journal. "I won't read it. And I don't want to talk about it anymore. I have forgiven Sylvester and I will try to forgive Susie Mae too, God helping me. But I can't handle any more," she choked.

Andrew looked at her compassionately. "I'll just say one more thing. When I left her, Susie Mae said to tell you she is sorry, and that she hasn't had a good night's sleep since she heard that Father died. She said she has been a terrible person."

Everyone was quiet. Then Bishop George spoke, "Why don't we pray. I think this is enough for one day."

Andrew did not read the final entry to his mother, written the day before Sylvester died:

I wonder if Susie Mae has left yet. I miss her already.

The Tree of Knowledge

*In the day ye eat thereof, then your eyes shall be opened,
and ye shall be as gods, knowing good and evil.*
—The serpent, the Book of Genesis

Several months later, on a bright Sunday morning in February, Bishop George preached a sermon that became known as "that sermon Bishop George preached." Andrew sensed from the beginning of the service that the bishop had something on his mind and that during the opening sermon, he seemed to be deep in thought. At first Andrew thought George was only tired, but by the time the bishop rose to preach, Andrew knew he was deeply concerned about something, rather than tired or depressed.

"I'd like to talk about two trees this morning," Bishop George started. "They are first mentioned in the second chapter of Genesis." He flipped in his Bible and read Genesis 2:9.

"Before Eve was created, God gave Adam clear instructions about the Tree of the Knowledge of Good and Evil. Man was not to eat the fruit of this tree, under pain of death. Apparently, they were free to eat from the Tree of Life as much as they wanted."

The bishop looked around the group. "Other than this one restriction, God allowed Adam and Eve to live as they wished. Since they had no knowledge of evil, they were innocent—just like a newborn baby is innocent. They didn't even know what sin or evil was.

"The entire world was innocent. There was no evil, no trouble, no sin of any sort. Nothing to be afraid of. No evil lurking in dark corners to attack the unwary. Even the animals appear to have been vegetarians and didn't kill each other." He paused and smiled at some of the younger children in the audience. "Can you imagine walking up to a lion or tiger and scratching it behind the ears like you do your kitty?"

The children listened wide-eyed. No, they couldn't imagine that.

Bishop George was already continuing. "Adam and Eve were walking past the Tree of the Knowledge of Good and Evil one day, when the serpent stopped them. Adam had named the serpent, and he had no reason to be afraid of it. I suspect they were startled to hear it talking to them, but they had no reason to expect that something evil had entered the world. So, they listened."

He paused for effect. "It was the worst thing they ever did. The serpent called their attention to the tree, and they noticed that it had delicious-looking fruit. It probably had attractive leaves and maybe even beautiful flowers. It really didn't look evil at all.

"The devil assured them they wouldn't die if they ate the fruit from the tree. God had ulterior motives, according to the serpent. He said God knew that if they ate that fruit, they would become like gods and would know good and evil, just like God did!"

Most preachers avoided conversational preaching as it was not considered reverent. But George wanted to make sure his audience got the point. "Sometimes people wonder why God put the tree there. But I think He wanted to test Adam and Eve, to see if they were really His friends. So He gave them a choice.

"The Tree of the Knowledge of Good and Evil seems to represent the pleasures of sin. You can't really get knowledge of evil without experiencing sin. That is what Adam and Eve didn't realize. They chose to eat the forbidden fruit because they expected it to taste good and fill them with a knowledge that would make them like God.

"But they paid a terrible price for that knowledge, because they had to stop eating from the tree of life. It was truly a life or death decision. You can't eat from both trees. If you want to enjoy the pleasures of sin, you give up life. If you want life, you must give up the pleasures of sin.

"Adam and Eve didn't enjoy that pleasure very long. They had barely tasted it before guilt flooded over them. They heard God coming and they hid from Him."

Here Bishop George paused again while the audience considered what he had been saying. "Just imagine. Up until that day, God had been their best friend. They had walked and talked with Him in the cool of the evening. Now they were in terror because He was coming.

"I wonder how God felt. We sometimes hurt people we love. But how often do we stop and think of how we hurt God? Jesus died for our sin, and we push that aside for a few minutes of pleasure. It doesn't even last more than a moment or two, then we face that horrible guilt again, and the knowledge of failure. And we grieve God, who gave the very best that heaven had to deliver us."

It was a heart-searching message. At the conclusion, he brought the focus closer to home.

"Sin is selfish," he said earnestly. "When we sin, we think only of ourselves and our pleasure. Yet our sin hurts those around us. It especially hurts those who love us. When we sin, we prove that we love ourselves more than God and more than our family.

"But there is one more thing we often forget: unbelievers will judge God and the church by our actions.

"You might think your actions are your own business. You might assume your thoughts won't damage anyone. But in the end, sin always hurts others. It hurts us too, but the real damage we do is in hurting innocent ones around us."

Bishop George closed his Bible. "Sin is not a personal matter.

God will judge us not only for our disobedience, but also for what our sin does to others."

Andrew and Selina left as soon after the service as they could. They had been planning to visit friends for lunch but changed their minds.

"I think I would rather go home," Andrew told Selina as they left the churchyard. "Somehow I don't feel like spending the afternoon in small talk after that message."

Selina nodded her agreement. "Did it bring back too many old memories?" she asked compassionately. "I'm sure Bishop George was thinking of your father, at least part of the time."

Andrew pondered her question for a bit. "It brought back memories," he admitted. "But not in the same way. I've gotten to the point of feeling sorry for my father rather than upset. But I could sure understand what Bishop George was talking about," he said feelingly.

He shook the reins, and the horse lengthened its stride. "I must admit that the idea of our sins affecting those around us was a new one to me, until last year. I wonder how many people have turned their backs on God, or Christianity, as a result of my father's actions." He guided the horse around the corner toward home. "Or, for that matter, how many people *my* life has influenced."

He was quiet for a few moments. "I keep thinking about Wes, for instance."

Selina looked at him questioningly. "You mean the gambler? Why?"

Andrew bit his lip. "I'm not sure. Not many people in town knew my father better than he did. He seems impressed at my mother's testimony, and I wonder if he would have been interested in a different kind of life if he hadn't run into my father."

"Maybe you should go talk to him," Selina said softly. "It couldn't do any harm, even if he isn't interested. At least he would know that you cared, even if your father didn't."

A few months later Andrew went to town to get some supplies. On an impulse, he decided to go into the saloon and see if Wes was there.

Again, he stood inside the door for a few moments while his eyes adjusted. He glanced toward the corner where Wes usually sat. There he was. The gambler had seen Andrew enter, and when he saw that Andrew noticed him, he jerked his thumb at the chair on the opposite side of the table.

Andrew sat down, and Wes motioned for the waitress. "Two cups of coffee," he said. "And make it stronger than last time. The stuff you brought us last time was like dishwater."

The waitress glanced at Andrew and nodded. "I'll brew a fresh batch," she promised. "Be a few minutes, though."

The two men looked each other over silently. The contrast in their appearance could have been the subject of a painting. The gambler had a week's growth of stubble on his face. His hair straggled over his ears, and an unlit pipe dangled from his mouth. He wore a dirty shirt and a tattered vest. His eyes were cold and hard and sin-seared. He had the look of a man who would destroy his best friend at a whim and not worry about it.

Andrew was young, and his eyes were bright and free from guilt. He was dressed neatly and his hair was combed. He had a beard, but not a scraggly one. Even the look on his face was different from the gambler's expression. Andrew was a man who cared, and the gambler could see it.

A few other customers came in, and a few went out. Most glanced curiously at the two men talking at the side table. Jim McCraw told his wife about it that night.

"Can't believe how that young Andrew Martin has grown up. I don't know what it is between him and that gambler, but he's a man, sure enough. Got a lot of his mom in him, that he does." And as an afterthought, "He sure is a sight different from Sylvester."

The waitress brought their coffee. It was good and strong this time, much better than dishwater. But neither of the men was really interested in the coffee.

"What's on your mind?" Wes asked bluntly. "Susie Mae has left town for keeps. So don't go looking for her."

Andrew took another sip of coffee. "I wasn't looking for Susie Mae," he said. "I just drove by and thought of you and wondered if you were here."

"And since I am?" Wes eyed him warily.

"I don't know," Andrew said frankly. "Maybe you would be interested in knowing that my mother is doing well and that she has forgiven Susie Mae and prays for her every day."

The gambler's eyes flickered a little. "What does that have to do with me?"

Andrew shrugged. "Maybe nothing. I just thought you might be interested, but maybe you aren't. In which case I'll thank you for the coffee and be on my way."

Wes was quiet, while Andrew watched his face. Finally, the gambler gave in. "Yes, I guess I am interested," he admitted slowly. "I've never before met the kind of Christian that your mother is. My mother died when I was born, and my father was your father's kind. He was a deacon in his church, but the biggest hypocrite you ever met. So I have an idea what you went through growing up. Only you made the opposite choice about it than I did. Maybe because you had a Christian mother and I didn't."

Andrew looked at him sympathetically. *So, we do have something in common, even though no one would know it.* "Have you ever considered going back and starting over?"

Wes looked at Andrew as if he had lost his mind. "Are you crazy? Any church I know would kick me out so fast I'd never get a chance to sit down."

He put up his hand to stop Andrew's answer. "Look, I appreciate you thinking of me. And I appreciate your mother. But it's too late for me. Besides I'm really not interested in what your father represented."

"How about what my mother represents?" Andrew persisted.

Wes grunted. "Of course, I'd be interested in that. But there are mighty few people like your mother in any church." He paused before adding, "Or like you. A lot more are like your father was, and he was no better than I am," he said emphatically.

Andrew got to his feet. "You know that my father kept a journal?"

Wes jerked his head. "I heard you talking to Susie Mae."

"Well, all his life he wanted to change his ways," Andrew said. "It is all through that journal, but he never got it done. Now it's too late. But until you take your last breath, it isn't too late for you. It doesn't have anything to do with church or other people. It has to do with you and God."

He looked Wes squarely in the eyes and added, "Don't do like my father did and wait until it's too late."

He turned and left. Wes watched him go, an inscrutable look on his face. Then he turned to the waitress sauntering by his table. "Get me a glass of whiskey."

The name of God is blasphemed among the Gentiles because of you (Romans 2:24).

Epilogue

Grass and bushes have overgrown the old graveyard today. Many of the old tombstones have toppled over. Most are illegible. But if you clear away some of the underbrush from what was once the fencerow, you can still find some graves with readable markers. Buried here are a man and his wife and an infant son. They have rested undisturbed for close to a century and a half.

All is quiet now. The old church is gone, and no one uses the old graveyard anymore. Occasionally a fox or a squirrel wanders through. But they do not disturb the deep slumber of the dead.

These are the forgotten ones. They have had their turn in this life and their earthly story has been told. They have made their choices.

This will be you some day.

> Just think, some night the stars will gleam
> Upon a cold grey stone,
> And trace a name with silver beam,
> And lo! 'twill be your own.
> —Robert W. Service, "Just Think!"

About the Author

Lester Bauman was born into an Old Order Mennonite home close to Kitchener, Ontario. Later, his family joined a local conservative Mennonite church. As a young-married man, he taught for five years in several Christian schools. Later, he worked for thirteen years out of a home office for Rod and Staff Publishers, Inc. as a writer and editor. During this time, he and his wife Marlene moved with their family from Ontario to Alberta, where they live presently. They have six children and ten grandchildren, and are members of a local Western Fellowship Mennonite Church.

During his time with Rod and Staff, Lester wrote ten books, including *The True Christian* and *God and Uncle Dale,* both available from Christian Aid Ministries. He spent a number of years in Alberta working as an HR manager in a corporate setting. He now works for the Christian Aid Ministries billboard evangelism ministry out of a home office, doing content writing for their website, answering correspondence, and writing resource materials.

Lester recently self-published a book based on Ecclesiastes titled,

Where Is God When Life Doesn't Make Sense. He is also working on several books for Christian Aid Ministries as he has time.

You can contact Lester through his personal website at www.lbauman.ca or by email at lester@lbauman.ca. You may also write to him in care of Christian Aid Ministries, P.O. Box 360, Berlin, Ohio 44610.

About Christian Aid Ministries

Christian Aid Ministries was founded in 1981 as a non-profit, tax-exempt 501(c)(3) organization. Its primary purpose is to provide a trustworthy and efficient channel for Amish, Mennonite, and other conservative Anabaptist groups and individuals to minister to physical and spiritual needs around the world. This is in response to the command to ". . . do good unto all men, especially unto them who are of the household of faith" (Galatians 6:10).

Each year, CAM supporters provide 15–20 million pounds of food, clothing, medicines, seeds, Bibles, Bible story books, and other Christian literature for needy people. Most of the aid goes to orphans and Christian families. Supporters' funds also help to clean up and rebuild for natural disaster victims, put up Gospel billboards in the U.S., support several church-planting efforts, operate two medical clinics, and provide resources for needy families to make their own living. CAM's main purposes for providing aid are to help and encourage God's people and bring the Gospel to a lost and dying world.

CAM has staff, warehouses, and distribution networks in Romania,

Moldova, Ukraine, Haiti, Nicaragua, Liberia, Israel, and Kenya. Aside from management, supervisory personnel, and bookkeeping operations, volunteers do most of the work at CAM locations. Each year, volunteers at our warehouses, field bases, Disaster Response Services projects, and other locations donate over 200,000 hours of work.

CAM's ultimate purpose is to glorify God and help enlarge His kingdom. ". . . whatsoever ye do, do all to the glory of God" (1 Corinthians 10:31).

The Way to God and Peace

We live in a world contaminated by sin. Sin is anything that goes against God's holy standards. When we do not follow the guidelines that God our Creator gave us, we are guilty of sin. Sin separates us from God, the source of life.

Since the time when the first man and woman, Adam and Eve, sinned in the Garden of Eden, sin has been universal. The Bible says that we all have "sinned and come short of the glory of God" (Romans 3:23). It also says that the natural consequence for that sin is eternal death, or punishment in an eternal hell: "Then when lust hath conceived, it bringeth forth sin: and sin, when it is finished, bringeth forth death" (James 1:15).

But we do not have to suffer eternal death in hell. God provided forgiveness for our sins through the death of His only Son, Jesus Christ. Because Jesus was perfect and without sin, He could die in our place. "For God so loved the world that he gave his only begotten Son, that whosoever believeth in him should not perish, but have everlasting life" (John 3:16).

A sacrifice is something given to benefit someone else. It costs the giver greatly. Jesus was God's sacrifice. Jesus' death takes away the penalty of sin for all those who accept this sacrifice and truly repent of their sins. To repent of sins means to be truly sorry for and turn away from the things we have done that have violated God's standards (Acts 2:38; 3:19).

Jesus died, but He did not remain dead. After three days, God's Spirit miraculously raised Him to life again. God's Spirit does something similar in us. When we receive Jesus as our sacrifice and repent of our sins, our hearts are changed. We become spiritually alive! We develop new desires and attitudes (2 Corinthians 5:17). We begin to make choices that please God (1 John 3:9). If we do fail and commit sins, we can ask God for forgiveness. "If we confess our sins, he is faithful and just to forgive us our sins, and to cleanse us from all unrighteousness" (1 John 1:9).

Once our hearts have been changed, we want to continue growing spiritually. We will be happy to let Jesus be the Master of our lives and will want to become more like Him. To do this, we must meditate on God's Word and commune with God in prayer. We will testify to others of this change by being baptized and sharing the good news of God's victory over sin and death. Fellowship with a faithful group of believers will strengthen our walk with God (1 John 1:7).